Gloria Loughman

R·A·D·I·A·N·T
LANDSCAPES

Transform Tiled Colors & Textures into Dramatic Quilts

C&T PUBLISHING

Text and Photography copyright © 2013 by Gloria Loughman

Photography and Artwork copyright © 2013 by C&T Publishing, Inc.

Publisher: Amy Marson

Creative Director: Gailen Runge

Art Director: Kristy Zacharias

Editor: Lynn Koolish

Technical Editor: Susan Nelsen and Mary E. Flynn

Cover/Book Designer: April Mostek

Production Coordinator: Jenny Davis

Production Editor: Alice Mace Nakanishi

Illustrator: Jenny Davis

Photography by Tony Loughman, unless otherwise noted

Published by C&T Publishing, Inc., P.O. Box 1456, Lafayette, CA 94549

Library of Congress Cataloging-in-Publication Data

Loughman, Gloria, 1949-

 Radiant landscapes : transform tiled colors & textures into dramatic quilts / Gloria Loughman.

    pages cm

  ISBN 978-1-60705-630-0 (soft cover)

  1. Patchwork. 2. Patchwork quilts. 3. Machine quilting. 4. Landscapes in art. I. Title.

  TT835.L696 2013

  746.46--dc23

                        2012025548

Printed in China

10 9 8 7 6 5 4 3 2

DEDICATION

I would like to dedicate this book to our much-loved grandchildren: Charlotte, Declan, Malachi, Lucy, Benjamin, Artemis, and Evie. The joy and richness you have brought to our lives have certainly been something very special.

I would also like to dedicate this book to the farming communities of Kerang, Murrabit, and Benjeroop, which were inundated with floodwater in early 2011 and are still on the long road back to recovery. Your strong spirit and determination, your endeavors to look after your neighbors, and your physical efforts have been inspirational.

ACKNOWLEDGMENTS

Thank you to C&T Publishing, yet again, for undertaking the publication of this book. To my friend and editor, Lynn Koolish, goes a special thank-you. Signing on for a third time takes amazing fortitude, and I really appreciate your expertise and patience.

I would also like to recognize my students, who have embraced the techniques in this book and have encouraged and supported me during the writing process. To the quilters whose work has been included in these pages, I owe a special thank-you. Your stunning quilts have added something very exciting and unique to this publication. I certainly value your contributions.

Thank you to my parents, Florence and Jack, for your love and positive encouragement.

Thank you also to our daughters, Amanda, Sarah, and Rebecca, who are always ready to be a sounding board and are very willing to give practical help and advice. I treasure the close relationship we share as a family.

And to my husband, Tony, what can I say? As photographer extraordinaire, you have made an outstanding contribution to this book. Your knowledge, expertise, and patience when photographing samples have been invaluable. Your folio of photos of our travels is exceptional, and I am very proud to include many of these photos as inspiration. I really value the time we have spent working together on this book and your infinite support for my endeavors.

Contents

Fern Pool by Gloria Loughman, 60″ × 74″ (154cm × 188cm)

L·O·O·K·I·N·G
AT LIGHT

I have always been drawn to the paintings of the impressionists. From Monet and Renoir to Cezanne and Van Gogh, their work has always held a fascination for me. I view their paintings as a visual feast through their efforts to capture light.

A visit to the Van Gogh museum in the Netherlands instilled in me a longing to create with color. Van Gogh painted with passion, concentrating on "painting the light." He liked to paint directly from nature, not caring whether his colors were true to nature, as long as the result looked beautiful on his canvas.

Light catches the eye. It pulls the viewer into a picture as it reveals the colors and shapes of the elements. When the light is just right, commonplace subjects are transformed and become noticed.

The sun and the moon are sources of natural light. The kind of light they produce varies from bright sunlight directly overhead on a clear day to just the barest hint of light coming from a sliver of the crescent of a new moon.

Light sets the mood. When the light is bright and overhead and the colors are strong and saturated, there is a feeling of warmth and energy. When the dominant color of the landscape is gray and the mist hovers in the trees, the mood is more mystical and mysterious.

Using light as a focus will make your work special. Light is a very important element, and it is crucial that you learn how to capture light in your work.

Showcase the light in your paintings by placing the greatest contrast between light and dark at the focal point. Limiting the amount of light and then focusing it on the important elements creates drama and impact.

The use of mosaic tiles echoes some of the work of the impressionists and the pointillists. Using brushstrokes or tiny dots of color, those artists were able to create a beautiful harmonious effect of gradual changes of color and value. Apparently, optical mixing occurs when the colors are not physically combined but are juxtaposed so that the eye is unable to differentiate individual colors from a distance. They are perceived as a rich mixture, having the average brightness of the component colors. They certainly have a special beauty and luminosity.

Tiling large areas of your quilts allows you, in some ways, to follow in these master painters' footsteps. By creating the tiles from a rich palette of colors and textures, you can gradually make changes in color and value, creating movement and interest. You can make the light flow around your design, weaving its magic.

Light just catches side of white lion's face.

Backlighting of setting sun in the White Desert of Egypt

H·O·W T·O U·S·E
THIS BOOK

Where do new ideas come from? Often events or images trigger a response, and our reaction is either to disregard this trigger or to embrace it, run with it, experiment with it, dream of it. This was my reaction to a small sample I made when writing *Quilted Symphony*. It was a small sample made with rectangles, placed at an angle over a dark background. Then the thought came: "This could make a great sky!" So the new journey began.

Using small tiles, rather than larger pieces of fabric, gives me the flexibility of incorporating many colors, values, and textures in one small area. I have been endeavoring for a long time to add the dimension of radiant light to my work. This is one way to make it possible.

Take the Journey

After you read the sections on design and color, reassess your fabric stash, searching out suitable fabrics. Perhaps you will be tempted to paint some fabric for yourself or to try dyeing. I can assure you that the mess and your efforts will be rewarded tenfold.

The section on design will help you create your own pattern, but if you want to try the techniques without making your own design, there are four projects included at the end of the book.

Once you have the pattern drawn out and have selected the fabrics, the chapters on construction will lead you through the process of tiling and building up the background. You might try tiling a sky, mountains, or a body of water. Indeed, you could tile the whole landscape for a beautiful effect.

The background segments are quilted as they are applied. So for this technique, the final step is to add foreground elements or surface decoration such as trees, figures, buildings, or any other image you would like to include.

There are many ways to finish the edges of a quilt. A faced edge has a contemporary feel to it, but some designs need more definition. A number of strategies, including a very narrow border, are presented.

I have really enjoyed using the tiling process in my own work. I am still thrilled and excited by the effects I can achieve with mosaic tiles. I hope you enjoy using these techniques and find that you can create your own stunning landscapes, full of radiant light.

D·E·S·I·G·N·I·N·G
YOUR QUILT

Diamond tiles in sky create tranquility.

Lakeside by Gloria Loughman, 22″ × 15″ (56cm × 38cm)

The first step in designing your quilt is to search for a place or scene that captures your attention. Some scenes actually jolt you into action. They reach out to you and almost demand to be featured.

I have found that many quilt artists seem almost supersensitive to their surroundings—they are always on the hunt for a subject to be explored, an idea to be tossed around, a scene to be interpreted. It is quite addictive and exhilarating to be always on the lookout for your next potential subject.

Sources of Inspiration

Inspiration is the starting point. It is that fire burning from within that ignites your desire to create an image. Sources of inspiration usually come from your heart rather than your head. Personality, experiences, preferences, and thoughts come into play. Go with your intuition, listening to your visual voice—the voice that draws you toward a particular image.

Sources of inspiration can be varied and diverse, as we each view our world in a different way. A rusty tin tank stand can be a cause of great excitement to one artist and something that needs disposing of for someone else.

TAKING PHOTOGRAPHS

Most artists draw their inspiration from the physical world around them, starting with what they see. Something about a scene triggers an emotional response—a response that leads to creating the image in their chosen medium. A painter may have the opportunity to sketch or even do a quick painting. As a textile artist, you have a much slower process, so luckily you can take digital photos for future reference. A small digital camera can be carried in your pocket almost anywhere, and now even phones can take good-quality images. So there is no excuse. Learn to take good photos so you have a number of quality images to refer to in the studio.

Photos provide a wonderful reference, but remember that they are just the starting place. Using the camera's viewfinder to compose a scene can be a great advantage, as is the opportunity to take a lot of shots and then delete the ones you don't want. Using some of the simpler software programs available to experiment with cropping and other editing strategies can be very useful as well.

Old, rusty tank

Detail of rich colors and textures

Collection of photos based on boat theme

USING A SKETCHBOOK

Use a sketchbook to create a visual record of your travels, images you love, unusual color schemes, thoughts, ideas—whatever you decide to include. It is a personal journal. Some sketchbooks are full of beautiful drawings, while others, like mine, have jottings, pictures cut from travel brochures, sketches, photographs, and color schemes. It is not something to place on show, but a very useful record and, better still, a place where you know to find things. Get in the habit of recording information, doing small sketches, and collecting your resources. It will go hand in hand with your photographic record and will help you remember your subject in detail.

The Design Process

BEGINNING THE DESIGN

Once you have a subject, it is time to interpret it in your own way. The photograph is the true image, and it is impossible to replicate this without feeling disappointed. Start the design process by asking yourself some questions:

- What is the main point of interest?

- What do I want to highlight?

- Do I want a realistic image or something more abstract?

- What color scheme do I want to use?

- Do I want to use the original colors or change the color scheme?

- Where is the darkest dark and the lightest light?

- How big do I want the finished quilt to be?

- Which view—portrait or landscape—do I want?

- What should be the proportion of length to width?

COMPOSITION

As you are planning your design, keep in mind some very important considerations. Composition is an organized arrangement of shapes that is pleasing to the eye and gives the design an order for the viewer to follow. A successful composition not only initially attracts the viewer to the image but also engages the viewer so that he or she will further study and enjoy the work. There are well-established principles of design (some of which are discussed below), but for any given project, some factors will be critical, and others will be less significant or not relevant at all.

You can edit any scene and make it more interesting by adding, subtracting, and changing shapes and angles. Change things as needed to achieve a pleasing result. No one will go back to the scene in the photo and hold up your design for comparison. So if you have to move a tree or change the shape of a bush, do so without feeling guilty. By the same token, always try to retain the integrity of the place and your response to it.

Once you have an image in mind, it is time to draw out your design. It is a good idea for a beginner, or even an experienced artist, to create thumbnail sketches before getting started. Once you are happy with the way your design is evolving, you can start work on the full-size drawing.

Simplify

The first step of design is learning to see and simplify the basic shapes of a subject so that they can be translated into a strong design. The structure of these basic background shapes forms the foundation of the design, and there can be literally thousands of bushes, trees, rocks, and more vying for attention. It is at this point that you should begin editing—deciding what to leave out as well as what to include. Handled correctly, the relationships between the large shapes give landscape designs the presence that makes them read well from a distance and prompts the viewer to take a closer look.

Evaluate the overall scene to make sure the big shapes can be identified; then organize them into an interesting structure. Specifically, try to compose the scene with three to five main shapes or masses. It is important to keep the background design simple—you will have the opportunity later to create areas featuring details and textures.

Beautiful scene in Yosemite National Park, California

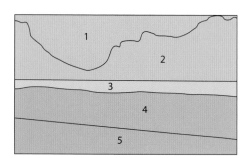

Draw main background shapes.

Balance

Balance is the distribution of the main elements of a design to achieve visual equilibrium. Balance can be symmetrical, which means the design is similar on either side of a central line, or asymmetrical. In landscapes, an asymmetric balance is usually more interesting and pleasing to the eye.

You can achieve this balance in a number of different ways. You can balance a large shape with a few smaller shapes. Repetition of colors and textures in different areas can also assist in developing balance. If you are striving for a realistic look, placing the heavier weight at the bottom can make the image look grounded. The weight can be actual or implied. Darker fabrics appear heavier, as do larger shapes. Taking the base of a tree out of the bottom of your design, or placing its base close to the bottom edge, can also help ground your work.

Large formation in foreground is balanced by two smaller formations in background (White Desert, Egypt).

Sometimes the heavier weight adds more drama when positioned at the top of a design. The heavier area becomes more important and dominant, adding some excitement and tension.

Darker background provides drama (Grand Mosque, Abu Dhabi).

When breaking up a background into its main areas, try not to place the horizon line dead center, as this will have a tendency to cut your work in half. Artists are often advised to place this line a third of the way from either the top or bottom edge. If the sky is to be tiled, then lower the horizon to a position that is noticeably lower than halfway. There is no set rule. The horizon line can be moved up or down depending on your design. In *Acid Rain* (below left), the horizon line is positioned very low.

High horizon line at sunset (Karumba, Australia)

Emphasis

What is your main point of interest? Most designs benefit from a strong point of interest or focal point. You need to establish a point, a place to draw the eye, a reward for the journey of traveling around through the design.

There are a number of ways to achieve this. You can use intense color, a line leading the eye to the focal point, or a strong contrast in value. A light object against a very dark background or vice versa will certainly draw the eye.

Low horizon line

Acid Rain by Gloria Loughman, 20″ × 60″ (51cm × 152cm)

Text and strong color draw the eye (Murrabit, Australia).

Line of canal leads the eye toward yellow building and church spire (Venice, Italy).

Light leaves of fern contrast with dark background (detail of *Fern Pool*; full quilt on page 4).

Placing the focal point off-center and balancing the weight with other objects will generally be much more effective than placing the main feature in the center. If possible, the focal point should be placed in a position that is a different distance from all sides of the picture. This isn't always possible; it depends on the design. If you have one large tree, it may call out to be positioned centrally in the design. If this is the case, try to have parts of the tree cross the central vertical axis, giving the design more visual interest.

Harmony

Harmony gives viewers a sense that the elements of the design belong together and are related. It is an important element of design, as it provides a sense of visual well-being.

Color choices are crucial to creating harmony. A vivid sunset sky will affect the color of a body of water and the foreground. When the sky is blue, the grass may be green and the tree trunks brown. At sunset, the grass might be mauve or orange and the trunks' silhouettes dark purple. The sky sets the scene, so it is important to work out the palette of the sky in advance.

Consistency of color and small value changes help create unity. When tiling a sky, subtle changes of color and value will give you a beautiful, cohesive background.

Another way of creating harmony is to place elements close to one another, even overlapping them. To provide some unity to a background, a tree that overlaps a number of the background areas will link the areas together.

Photo by Nigel Fearon Photography

Subtle changes of color in sky

Evening Tranquility by Donna M. MacDonald, 22″ × 34″ (56cm × 86cm)

Contrast

Trying to provide unity can sometimes result in boredom. Contrast makes a work exciting. Use intense colors against neutral colors, warm colors against cool colors, diagonal lines against vertical lines. Consider opposites such as large against small, textured against smooth, and—always a sensation—light against dark. As discussed earlier (page 5), light is a very powerful ingredient. Sometimes the placement of a touch of light produces a very powerful effect on a dark background. If the actual light source is not where you want it, put it where you would like it to be. Often, changing or adding light will improve the balance and flow of the design and make it more effective.

Evening light on sculpture (Broken Hill, Australia)

Visual Movement

When you arrange shapes for a quilt design, think about the emotions you are hoping to stir in your viewers.

Vertical lines imply strength and are usually man-made, such as buildings, fences, bridges, light poles, and so on.

Strong vertical lines of skyscrapers (Dubai)

Horizontal lines give a feeling of calmness and peace. Reflect on the horizontal lines of a lake on a very still day.

Horizontal lines on tranquil water (Tin Can Bay, Australia)

If you want to add more excitement to your design, take inspiration from nature, which is full of directional movement. Diagonal lines bring energy and movement to a design. Usually the eye is guided from light to light, jumping across spaces. Take advantage of lines that lead the eye into the design, and leave out elements that lead to the outer side edge and out of the quilt before the viewer has had time to appreciate the work.

Take advantage of lines that lead into the design (Leichhardt River, Australia).

Also provide quieter areas where the viewer's eye can rest. Space in a design is necessary to give the eye room to travel around and then rest awhile before being drawn back to the most exciting part, the focal point.

Graduated changes of color in a tiled area can provide a gentle area of movement that doesn't compete with the focal point. It will read as one space but will provide interest and subtle contrast.

Texture

Texture is influenced by the direction of light and the surface texture of the subject. Textured surfaces surround us, particularly in nature, where they are evident on rocks, the bark of trees, sand, and water.

Wonderful texture of peeling paint on rusty corrugated iron

Many commercial fabrics can help you create beautiful texture in your designs. You can also use paint and stitching to build up levels of interest and detail. Texture invites the viewer to step in to have a closer look at the richness of the surface.

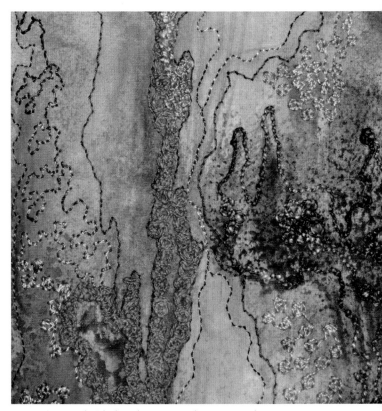

Texture is created with thread on tree trunks in *Fern Pool* (full quilt on page 4).

DEPTH—CREATING PERSPECTIVE

When designing, you quickly become aware of space, especially when you are trying to create the illusion of depth in a landscape while working with fabric on a flat surface.

The illusion of depth is made possible by positioning objects far and near. Objects appear to grow smaller the further away they are. By placing large and small versions of the same object in a design, you suggest space and depth.

Fence posts appear smaller in distance.

Objects overlapping in the visual field create an illusion of foreground, middle ground, and background. Overlapping suggests that one object is behind the other and implies that there must be depth in the picture.

Another point to remember is that the amount of detail you are able to see depends on how close you are to an object. At a distance, you can see less detail. Thus, the fabrics used in the background need to be blurred and indistinct in comparison to the more detailed and textured fabrics used for the foreground.

When considering design features such as rivers, roads, and buildings, remember that the lines appear to converge as they move away from you. When struggling with a drawing of a building, I sometimes isolate the structure in my photograph and then photocopy it to enlarge it up to size, retaining the perspective that is crucial to the design. It's important to work from your own photos, so you are not breaking any copyright laws.

Lines of buildings and canal converge in distance (Venice, Italy).

Color choices also help create depth. Refer to Color and Perspective (pages 43 and 44).

LANDSCAPE OR PORTRAIT VIEW

The decision to work in portrait or landscape view certainly has an impact on the composition of an image. Choose the format that reflects your subject's general linear direction to maximize the visual impact of your design.

The landscape view naturally conforms to the horizon and is the obvious choice for many scenes. The horizontal frame sits well with a horizontal arrangement of elements.

Photo by Sarah Murray

Hay bales along fence line suit horizontal format.

A design with a strong vertical element will be more effective set in a portrait or vertical format. Having a passion for tree photography, I am aware of how difficult it sometimes is to capture tall trees in the lens without shooting upward. Using the vertical format, which echoes the shape of the tree, means you can showcase most of the tree at a close enough distance to retain the texture and the tree's other idiosyncrasies.

Designs that feature tall buildings or figures may also work better in a vertical format.

Original photo (Okavango Delta, Botswana)

Cropped to suit vertical format (Okavango Delta, Botswana)

Vertical format suits tall sequoia trees (California).

You don't have to retain the format of the original photograph. Consider the linear direction of the subject and change the view if you think it will make your image more powerful.

QUILT SIZE AND PROPORTION

Sometimes your decisions about the size and the length-to-width ratio of a quilt are governed by where you plan to hang the quilt when it is completed. To make the best of your design, choose the ratio that works best for the composition. A square quilt does not usually allow for directional movement to be a feature, so consider 1:2, 1:3, 1:4, 3:4, or even 2:3 to give that extra space.

TIP •

For more detailed information on scale and proportion, refer to *Adventures in Design* by Joen Wolfrom. Her Magic Design-Ratio Tool makes it easy to implement your proportion decisions.

Horizontal 1:3 ratio (White Desert, Egypt)

REALISTIC OR ABSTRACT?

Over time, artists tend to develop their own style. This growth as an artist is not easy. The transition is not always smooth, but it's something fluid that ebbs and flows. My own journey started with realistic landscape; then I moved into my abstract period, concentrating on pattern and shape. Now I am combining the two, experimenting with my style of abstract landscape.

When you are not limited to a literal image, the important thing is to still retain the essence of your subject. When attempting to faithfully reproduce a scene, you work hard at producing a three-dimensional–looking form. Abstract design allows you to reverse values and color temperatures, change shapes, discard converging lines, or eliminate parts or all of the background and foreground. Nothing in your design needs to be real.

Vertical 1:3 ratio (waterfall in Yosemite National Park, California)

The relationship between realistic and abstract is a continuum, and many successful artists retain some realistic elements while playing around with others.

My eldest granddaughter, Charli, created a special landscape with a celebration of circles in the background. It still reads as a landscape because of the recognizable form of the tree, yet the background has become a magical ambiguous space.

If you decide to tile areas of your quilt, you have taken some small steps down the continuum toward abstract design. You can stay at this station and work hard to create perspective, or you can travel farther. The length of the journey is up to you.

Charli's Quilt by Charli Bakker, 20″ × 14″ (51cm × 36cm)

Designing with Tiles

Most of the information about design presented earlier in this chapter is relevant for any art form, including painting, photography, and textiles. The following are design considerations specific to creating tiled landscapes.

There are countless options for the size and shape of tiles. They can be constant in shape and size, they can be a regular geometric shape, or they can be asymmetrical. You can vary the size but keep the shape constant, and you can place them on an angle or in a vertical or horizontal direction.

CHOOSING SEGMENTS TO BE TILED

Your first decision is to decide which area of the quilt you are going to tile. Constructing the Background (pages 57–74) outlines many options, including tiling a sky, a forest, mountains, a body of water, or even the whole background.

The area to be tiled must be a larger area of the background. It would be difficult to maintain harmony if a small area was tiled and the rest of the background was left plain; this would draw attention to the small area of the background rather than keeping the emphasis on the focal point. A large sky, with the horizon line low in the picture, is an obvious choice. You can create something very special with just a few elements in the foreground as a focus. The richness of the palette you create, with gradual variations of color and texture, ensures a beautiful and stunning outcome.

Rectangles

Some tile shapes work better than others when representing different areas of the landscape. There are no rules, but I find that the rectangle works well for foliage in the background and provides very strong directional movement when used in the sky on an angle.

Diagonal rectangles provide movement.

The Burmis Tree by Kay D. Gould, 26″ × 18″ (66cm × 46cm)

Diamonds

Diamonds work well if you want to create horizontal direction in your design. A serene lake, a peaceful sky, or distant hills can be replicated using diamonds. You have various options for placement, although to echo the horizontal feel, place them with the widest part across the design. *Lakeside* (page 8) is a good example of how diamonds can create tranquility.

Vertical rectangles

Colorado Aspens by Jan Sheets, 24″ × 32″ (61cm × 81cm)

Squares

Squares are more neutral and can work well for almost anything except water. They tend to be too deep to give the horizontal linear effect of water. Always place squares on point so the edges appear blurred and the colors flow across the surface.

BUILDING A BRIDGE

When placing tiles, look for those special bridging fabrics that allow you to make a smooth transition from one color or texture to the next. If you want to make the transition of blue to yellow, you will need some blue-green, green, and yellow-green fabrics to ensure a smooth transition. If you are using a multicolored hand-dyed or painted fabric, treasure those areas that feature an overlap of colors.

When all the tiles are in place, stand back and squint to see whether there are sharp edges or rogue tiles that need to be changed.

LIGHT SOURCE

Light plays an important role in design (page 5), but when placing tiles, you need to have already decided where the light source is positioned. In a sunset or sunrise sky, the light source will be low, close to the horizon line. As you place the tiles, think about the brightest part of the sky and position the tiles accordingly.

"When an artist is alive in any person whatever his kind of work may be, he becomes an inventive, searching, daring, self-expressing creature. He becomes interesting to other people. He disturbs, upsets, enlightens and he opens up ways for a better understanding. Where those who are not artists are trying to close the book, he opens it, shows there are still more pages possible."

—*From* The Art Spirit: Notes, Articles, Fragments of Letters and Talks to Students, Bearing on the Concept and Technique of Picture Making, the Study of Art Generally, and on Appreciation *by Robert Henri (Basic Books, 1984)*

PERSPECTIVE

The sky is lighter in color toward the horizon. Establish the darkest and lightest tiles to be featured and position them accordingly. Whether the sky is blue, gray, or a vivid strata of colors at sunset, the sky will be lighter toward the horizon.

EXPERIMENT

The quilts in this book mostly feature tiles that are regular in shape, but, of course, there are no rules. Play with circles, octagons, hexagons, or random mosaic shapes. Instead of leaving gaps between the tiles, try overlapping them. Try larger mosaic shapes. This is just the start. It is an adventure.

Photo by C&T Publishing

Larger mosaic shapes featured.

The Bristlecone Pine by Irma Lübbe, 31″ × 42″ (79cm × 107cm)

E·X·P·L·O·R·I·N·G
COLOR

Color can be enjoyed by anyone. You don't have to know anything about drawing or color theory to appreciate the superb colors of a magnificent sunset sky, the rich patina of faded colors on an old building, the spectacle of harmonizing and clashing colors in a marketplace, or the vivid contrast of an orange desert against a brilliant blue sky.

Split complementary colors

Cypress at Portarlington by Gloria Loughman, 20″ × 40″ (51cm × 102cm)

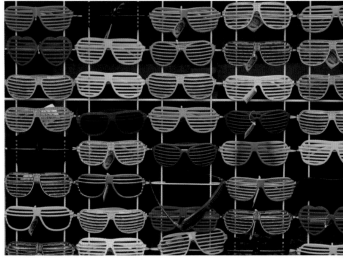

Shades of many colors

Marketplace (Stockholm, Sweden)

Color is probably the most expressive and emotional element of design. We all react to color in different ways, with some preferring wild, off-the-wall bold colors, while others prefer more sophisticated, subtle color schemes.

Effective use of color can turn something ordinary into something quite extraordinary. Being able to interpret what you see in your own unique way involves a combination of knowledge and intuition. A few fortunate people have a natural sense of color, but for most of us this sense requires a commitment to developing knowledge and sensitivity in combination with our instinctive ability. For those who have the motivation to explore color, a beautiful world awaits you.

For many artists, color is the most seductive aspect of their craft, be it painting, photography, or textiles. It can also be the most confusing and challenging aspect. Understanding the properties of color and studying some color schemes will give you a base on which to build. Experimenting, discovering, and creating come next. Learning color takes time. It is a journey—but far from arduous and boring, it is a journey full of exploring, creating, and having fun. Start tentatively and then take bigger steps, using your own instinct to identify what excites and appeals to you.

Remember, you don't have to use realistic or real-life color schemes. You have opportunities, if you accept them, to push colors to another level. Your individual color choices, your own bold statement and distinctive color style, make your artwork uniquely your own.

"I study nature so as not to do foolish things … I don't care so much whether my color is exactly the same, as long as it looks beautiful on my canvas."

—Vincent van Gogh

Sunset (South Africa)

Sand dunes (Namibia)

Old Town (Stockholm, Sweden)

This chapter presents two different yet related approaches for choosing color schemes. The first approach is to build a foundation by taking up the challenge of developing a base of knowledge and information. We will investigate the terms *hue*, *value*, *intensity*, and *temperature*. We will then look at the color wheel and explore color schemes that give us harmony and contrast. We will be building up color schemes.

The second approach is to start with a fabric or picture and use that as a starting point. If it improves the visual image, you can add to or subtract from the scheme using the knowledge you gained from the beginning of this chapter.

The Language of Color

Artists use accepted words to describe the properties of color. *Hue* is the name of the color, *value* is its lightness or darkness, and *intensity* is its purity or grayness. *Color temperature*, the warmth or coolness of a color, is also a critical element. Don't get bogged down with the jargon. As you explore color and increase your perception, being familiar with these terms will assist you in understanding and describing specific color characteristics and relationships.

HUE

Hue is the name of the color on the color wheel. Most color wheels are based on the three *primary colors* of yellow, red, and blue.

The *secondary colors* are mixed from the primaries, yielding green, violet, and orange. The third group is the *tertiary colors*, which are mixtures of two adjacent primary and secondary colors. Hence we have yellow-green, blue-green, blue-violet, red-violet, red-orange, and yellow-orange. Some people view the color wheel with trepidation, believing it involves complicated theories and complex rules, but I find the wheel a very useful tool and refer to it often. I carry a small version in my handbag when searching out fabrics, and my large wheel, the one I use in the studio, is spattered with paint and dye from constant use.

I find it helpful to always orient my color wheel with yellow, the lightest color, at the top. This means that violet, the darkest color, will be at the bottom.

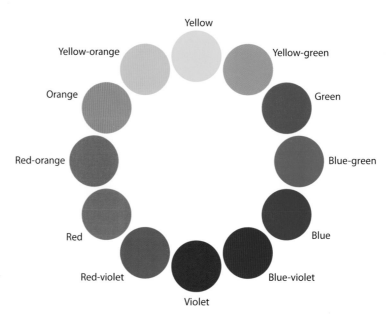

Color wheel with twelve hues

Color Tools

Joen Wolfrom's Ultimate 3-in-1 Color Tool and the Studio Color Wheel (both by C&T Publishing) are color-planning tools that can help you choose effective color combinations. See Resources (page 127).

VALUE

Value is the degree of lightness or darkness in a color. You can create tints by adding white and shades by adding black. Yellow is the lightest color; it becomes very light with just a bit of white added. Violet is the darkest, so when black is added, it becomes very dark very quickly. All the other colors are in between. Red and green are similar in value.

This book contains frequent references to value. Having a good understanding of value will help you create perspective. Value is also a key element for creating contrast or unity, thus adding drama or harmony to your work.

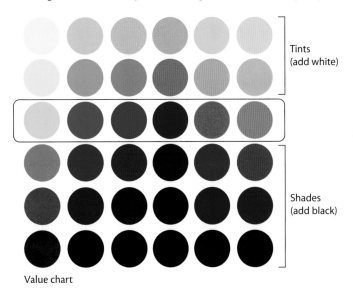

Value chart

Some colors retain their identity longer than others. Blue remains blue no matter how dark it becomes, whereas yellow becomes olive green and orange becomes brown.

INTENSITY

The intensity of a color (sometimes called chroma or saturation) is its brightness or dullness. Intensity depends on how pure the color is. A pure color has high intensity, and a grayed-down color has low intensity. To lower the intensity, you can mix a bright color with gray, black, or another muddy color. Varying the intensity can give you wonderful contrast or emphasis.

Red mixed with varying shades of gray and brown

TEMPERATURE

Color temperature helps create depth, movement, and mood. Warm colors are aggressive and appear to advance. Cool colors are passive and seem to recede.

Red-orange is the warmest color; as you move around the color wheel away from it, the colors become progressively cooler until you reach blue-green, the coolest color. Check this out on your color wheel.

Color temperature is relative. A color that appears warm in one context may look cool in another. It just depends on its neighbor.

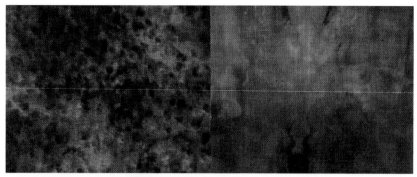

Violet appears warm next to blue.

Violet appears cool next to red.

It is interesting that within one hue, colors also have many temperatures. Consider yellow—it is generally accepted as a warm color. Yellows that tend toward green will seem much cooler than those that are more on the orange side.

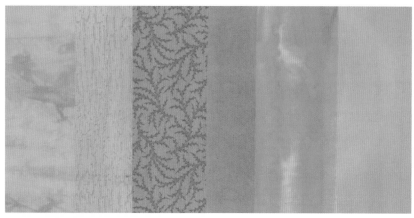

Cool and warm shades of yellow

While wandering through galleries and museums, open your eyes to color. While browsing through books on art or photography, record your reactions to colors in your journal. Build up a reference library of colors with your own digital photos of buildings featuring unique color schemes, old machinery faded and full of rust, and other images in which the color talks to you.

Left in the paddock to rust (Lightning Ridge, Australia)

Rich texture of old barn wall (Gamblesby, England)

Marketplace (Cairo, Egypt)

Mixing Colors for Painting Fabric

Painting fabric for a quilt can be very enjoyable, and it enables you to create the perfect color for your landscape. Painting techniques are described in Painting Fabric (pages 55 and 56), and there are many paint options available (see Resources, page 127).

You don't need to go to the expense of buying a lot of colors. It is fun and exciting to mix your own, and you'll learn more about color along the way.

Make sure you have the three primary colors of yellow, blue, and red, plus back and white. I also have a golden yellow and a violet. I haven't purchased green, as I find I can make a beautiful range of greens using my two yellows in combination with blue or black.

TINTS AND SHADES

To make a lighter color, simply add white. But sometimes you can add a whole tube of white, and the color will still not be light enough. You have much more control if you start with some white paint and add a small amount of color.

To make a darker shade, start with the color and add small amounts of black until it is dark enough. A small amount of black goes a long way, so do not add very much at a time.

MIXING OTHER COLORS

Now that you have mastered the tints and the shades, it is time to move on to mixing other colors for the landscape. You can look at the color wheel to work out that orange is a combination of yellow and red, but how do you make sand color, peach for a sunset, or a beautiful turquoise to paint sea fabric?

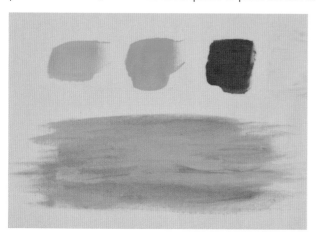

Mix sand color from white, yellow, and violet.

Make peach by beginning with white and adding a little yellow and a smidge of red.

Make a beautiful sea color by beginning with white and adding some blue and just a touch of yellow.

Intense brown is made by adding black to orange.

Another full-bodied brown is made by mixing yellow and violet.

Rich olive green is made by adding a touch of black to golden yellow.

Bright green is made by adding blue to yellow.

Remember that reproducing exact colors from nature is extremely difficult and often impossible.

"I wanted to copy Nature. And I failed."

—Cezanne

Don't be too hard on yourself. Enjoy the fun of painting. It is emotionally a wonderful thing to do. Take yourself back to kindergarten and enjoy the hands-on experience. Play with the colors. You will be amazed at the results. Some pieces of fabric I have painted didn't work out and were not used for their intended purpose. Ironed and folded in the drawer, they are sure to be used in projects yet to come. Think of fabric painting as another stash-building exercise. Your friends will be envious of your one-of-a-kind, never-to-be-repeated stunning fabrics.

There is much more information in Painting Fabric (pages 55 and 56).

Color Schemes

Color schemes are based on either harmony or contrast. The color schemes that feature similar colors are either monochromatic (one color in different values) or analogous (colors that are adjacent on the color wheel). Contrasting color schemes are generally based on complementary or triadic combinations.

One color is usually dominant in a color scheme, and you have multiple options as to which colors you add to it.

Looking at the color wheel, there are hundreds of possible combinations. Some you will love and others you will hate. Some schemes you may initially reject, but then as you become more confident they could well become your favorites. Take time to experiment and play with color schemes to see what you like. Take risks and try out unusual combinations. Having a knowledge and understanding of color schemes will actually challenge you to be more daring and adventurous as you develop confidence in your own color choices.

Color scheme based on harmony

Parisian Promenade by Jan Rowe, 24″ × 20″ (61 cm × 50cm)

Color scheme based on contrast

Birch Stand—Autumn by Nancy Trowbridge, 33″ × 14″ (84cm × 36cm)

Photo by C&T Publishing

MONOCHROMATIC

A monochromatic scheme features one color in different values, so it is quite simple in some ways but can be very powerful. This color scheme often evokes emotion in a viewer.

For example, a red color scheme can be exciting and animated, while a blue or green one can be very serene and peaceful. Black, gray, and white, an *achromatic* (without color) scheme, can be very dramatic. Compare the mood created in each of these pictures.

Run of blue from light to dark

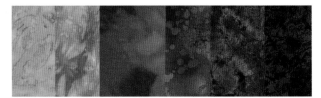

Monochromatic red-violet fabrics

Monochromatic color scheme (mountain range in Yosemite National Park, California)

For monochromatic color schemes to be effective, they must contain a contrast in values. If the scene contains all similar values, the effect will be bland and uninspiring, but one with contrast will be dynamic and will make us sit up and take notice.

Achromatic color scheme (Emerald Lake, Canada)

ANALOGOUS

Another color scheme based on similarity is the analogous color scheme. One of the easiest combinations to use, this scheme is made up of three or four different colors that are adjacent to each other on the color wheel. It could be a run of orange through red to violet for something regal and full of energy. A run of violet through blue to blue-green could evoke calmness and relaxation.

Using a palette of fully saturated colors will give a very different effect than using a palette of tints. Yet both schemes provide a harmony and unity that is very appealing to the viewer. As the colors are adjacent on the wheel, there is less chance of discord or friction, with the colors melding

together. Analogous colors enhance each other if you work in subtle graduations. Thus, they are a wonderful palette for mosaic tiles, as the colors gradually change from one to the next. Try to limit the number of different colors to four rather than working further around the color wheel to the contrasting fabrics.

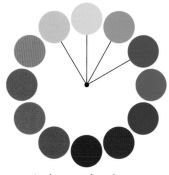

Analogous color schemes

Analogous run of warm colors: yellow to red

Analogous run of cool colors: green to blue

Analogous colors

Boabs in a Darwin Sunset by Ann Cox, 24″ × 21″ (61cm × 53cm)

Analogous colors

Shepherd's Delight by Shirley Sparks, 23″ × 19″ (58cm × 48cm)

COMPLEMENTARY

The first contrasting color scheme to explore uses two colors that are opposite each other on the color wheel. These two colors appear brighter and stronger when positioned side by side than when they are apart. When two complementary colors are mixed together, they produce a range of fabulous muddy or neutral colors. A range of these muddy colors juxtaposed with varying amounts of the pure colors provides a wonderful palette for any design.

Another alternative is to create contrast using the color next to the complement. This color scheme is definitely worth further exploration. Instead of using yellow and violet, try yellow and blue-violet or yellow and red-violet for a stunning color scheme.

Complementary color schemes can certainly deliver striking contrasts, but there are a few things to keep in mind. Make sure that one color is dominant. If both colors are used in the same proportions, there will be visual competition, and the design will suffer. By using a smaller proportion of the complementary color as a sharp accent, you create a more vibrant and powerful effect.

You can also use variations of value and chroma to moderate the intensity of the contrast to your liking.

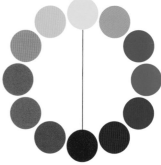

Complementary color schemes

Complementary scheme of yellow and violet

Complementary colors of yellow and violet
....
Last Light by Gloria Loughman, 24″ × 18″ (61cm × 46cm)

Complementary colors of yellow-orange and blue-violet
....
Tranquility by Prue Wheal, 27″ × 21″ (69cm × 53cm)

Split Complementary

Our second color scheme featuring contrast is split complementary. This combination is made up of three colors: a main color and the colors on either side of its complement. If you select red and then add yellow-green and blue-green, you will have a wonderful color scheme with striking contrasts between the near complements and some harmony between the two colors positioned close together on the wheel. Having a third color gives extra dimension and allows for additional shades to be incorporated into the design.

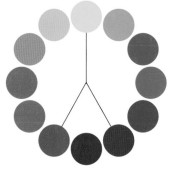

Split complementary color scheme

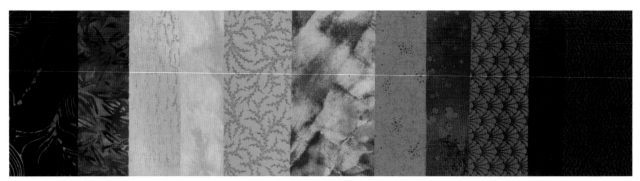

Split complementary fabrics: yellow with red-violet and blue-violet

Orange, blue-violet, and blue-green fishing nets provide vivid color in harbor.

Analogous Complementary

For the analogous complementary color scheme, combine an analogous group of colors with the complement of one of those colors. This color scheme allows you to use more colors, but it is important to establish the relationship between them. This scheme is usually very successful, as it has both harmony and contrast. The analogous colors create the dominant mood, and the complement provides the magical ingredient. You can choose any of the three complements, or more than one if you like, but make sure that the analogous range of colors is dominant.

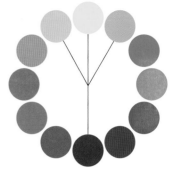

Analogous complementary schemes

Analogous fabrics of yellow-orange, yellow, and yellow-green teamed with blue-violet

Analogous complementary colors

Road to California Runner by Maggie Stimson, 31″ × 50″ (79cm × 127cm)

Analogous complementary colors

Sunset over Mountain Lake by Susan Mitchell, 20″ × 25″ (51cm × 64cm)

TRIADIC

Triads are based on the firm relationship that exists between three colors that are equal distances apart on the color wheel. There are only four triadic color schemes: one made up of primary colors, another made up of secondary colors, and two made up of tertiary colors. The primary triad is bold and attention grabbing. The secondary triad is more subtle and natural. The tertiary triads are wonderful combinations for the more adventurous. One color of the triad should be dominant, with another color taking a secondary role and the third a minor role. Remember that you have tints and shades as well as mixes of the colors to experiment with.

Primary triad of yellow, blue, and red fabrics

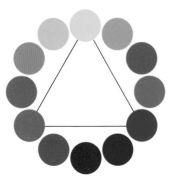 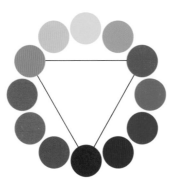

Primary triad of yellow, blue, and red · Secondary triad of green, violet, and orange

Secondary triad of orange, green, and violet fabrics

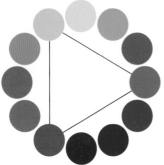

Tertiary triads of (*left*) blue-green, red-violet, and yellow-orange and (*right*) yellow-green, blue-violet, and red-orange

Tertiary triad tints of red-violet, blue-green, and yellow-orange fabrics

Triadic colors

Twilight by Gloria Loughman, 17″ × 23″ (43cm × 58cm)

Complementary Triadic

A modified version of the triad is the complementary triad. Select any two complements and then add one of the colors situated halfway between them. You could choose yellow and violet, and then add either red-orange or blue-green. The contrasts of the complements are exciting, and the third color adds a special accent. You are in fact using colors from one side of the color wheel, while introducing more contrast than in an analogous color scheme.

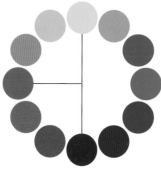

Complementary triadic color scheme

Yellow and its complement, violet, with blue-green

Yellow and its complement, violet, with red-orange

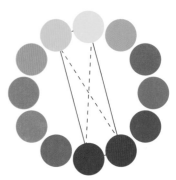

TETRADIC

The tetradic color scheme is made up of two sets of complementary colors. This four-color combination can form a square or rectangle on the color wheel. A rectangle is formed if the pairs are adjacent or if there is one color between. When there are two colors between, the complementary pairs form a square. The tetradic color scheme produces strong contrast, so having one color family as dominant and the others playing a supporting role will assist in bringing unity to this combination.

Rectangle tetradic color scheme

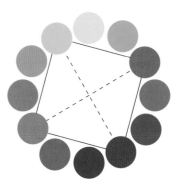

Square tetradic color scheme

Complementary triad of orange and blue with highlight of yellow-green

Ghost Gum on a Rocky Outcrop by Jeannie Henry, 12″ × 16″ (31cm × 41cm)

Complementary triad of blue and brown with yellow-green highlights

Oh How Lovely Was the Morning by Pauline M. Kacher, 32″ × 21″ (81cm × 53cm)

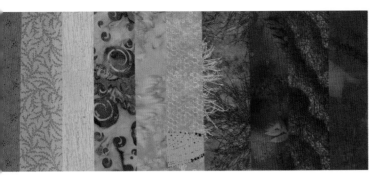

Adjacent rectangle tetrad of yellow and yellow-green with complements of violet and red-violet

Square tetrad of yellow and blue-green with their complements of violet and red-orange

PURE COLOR AGAINST A NEUTRAL BACKGROUND

Our final contrasting color scheme consists of a pure color set against neutral gray, white, or black. This scheme is widely used in advertising, as it is dynamic and eye-catching. Its strong graphic image makes a bold statement. To create high contrast, use a very light or dark background. For a more subdued look, try a gray background.

Wind Power by Gloria Loughman, 29" × 32" (74cm × 81cm)

NOTE • • • • • • • • •
Color schemes give you a foundation on which to build. But don't be daunted by feeling that you need to remember all the theory before you can start experimenting. Review the schemes with your color wheel in hand. Work out a few combinations for each of the schemes. You can make small sketches using colored pencils, samples of fabrics, or paint to see which combinations you prefer. Look at paintings and quilts you find appealing, noting the combinations and proportions of colors used. See if you can work out which color schemes were used. As you become more familiar with the different combinations, you will be equipped with the knowledge and understanding to produce quilts using new color schemes that are harmonious and dynamic.

A Different Starting Point

A fabulous length of fabric, a stunning photograph, a painting, a favorite dress, or even graffiti can act as a trigger or starting point for selecting color combinations. Starting with a color scheme you see, rather than imagine, is appealing to many quilt artists. In this section we will look at this alternative road, one that will take you on a journey to producing work that you feel confident will be appealing.

Your starting point could be a piece of fabric that contains a wonderful mix of colors. Your palette of colors is set, and you can add more fabric that blends and offers variety in value and intensity. Alternatively, perhaps the fabric that you want to include has a limited palette and you need to add more colors to achieve the result you are after.

This section looks at a number of projects using different starting points and shows you how to select additional fabrics to provide the contrast or unity you are after.

STARTING POINT 1— MULTICOLORED FABRIC

Initial fabric: rich orange, browns, and a touch of mustard

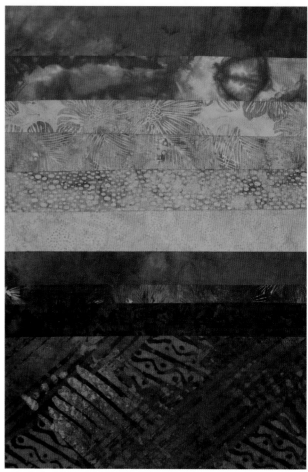

Initial fabric with additional fabrics to create sky and land areas

STARTING POINT 2—A DIFFERENT MULTICOLORED FABRIC

Initial fabric: beautiful blue-green fabric with a touch of yellow

Initial fabric with additional fabrics

STARTING POINT 3— LIMITED-PALETTE FABRIC

Initial fabric: soft red-violet and peach tones

Initial fabric with similar-colored fabrics plus yellow-green complementary fabric

STARTING POINT 4— A PHOTOGRAPH

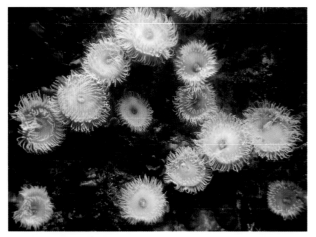

Mint green sea urchins against red-violet background

Fabrics based on colors in photo

STARTING POINT 5— A QUILT

Color Play by Gloria Loughman, 16″ × 21″ (41cm × 53cm)

Fabrics included are orange, yellow, greens, blue-greens, and tree in dark teal.

When you begin a project, you can design the quilt and then look for a color scheme or, alternatively, decide on the color scheme independent of the design. Instinct and intuition then will come into play to make it work. This second way of working will mean that your color schemes will be far from realistic, but they will certainly be original and compelling.

Color and Perspective

We've looked at many exciting color combinations, from realistic to way off the planet. We can't leave this section on color without looking at the way color contributes to creating perspective in our landscapes.

USING COLOR TO CREATE VISUAL DEPTH

Just like a magician creates illusions, you can also perform magic by manipulating your colors to create perspective.

Having a good understanding of value is critically important when creating depth. Features in the background will be washed out and faded. The colors in the foreground will have much more intensity. Hills in the background will appear washed out and will take on the color of the sky. On a day when the sky is blue, the hills will become bluer and more faded further into the background. At sunrise or sunset, they will pick up the glow of the beautiful colors in the sky. On a gray day, they will become grayer and lighter in color the farther they are in the distance.

Hills become paler as they recede into background (Port Douglas, Australia).

Depth can also be accentuated by placing the strongest sky colors visually closer to the viewer. The sky is normally a more intense color overhead and lighter near the horizon. This change of color is quite noticeable in a photograph, even when the sky seems to be a uniform blue.

Sky is lighter closer to horizon (Namibia).

Placing warm colors in the foreground and cool in the background is another way of creating an illusion of space. Warm colors tend to advance in comparison to cool colors. Reserve warm colors and strong contrasts in tone for the foreground. Adding a touch of red or orange to any color will make it come forward, and adding a touch of white, blue, or green will make it recede. If you do want to use yellows, oranges, or reds in the background, tone them down by mixing them with their complementary color or gray.

SKY COLORS

The sky sets the mood for everything else in the composition and is usually the lightest segment. Whatever colors you choose, when you place the sky fabric in the position of the sky in your quilt, it will read as sky. It could be green, orange, purple, or all three colors and it will still read as sky. Remember that there are occasionally skies that look so surreal you are afraid to put them in your landscape because you don't think people will believe them. Take the risk. As long as the colors of the landscape work in harmony with the sky, it will be credible.

WATER COLORS

Water is a magical element to include in a landscape. Having no color of its own, it reflects the colors of the elements around it. The main source of the water's color is the sky, although water is usually darker in tone. It is more faded closer to the horizon and more intense in color as it approaches the foreground.

Sky color reflected in floodwaters (Murrabit, Australia)

Water reflecting elements around it

Foreground colors are in harmony with sky.

"The Impressionist sits on the bank of a river. The water takes on every possible hue, according to the state of the sky, the perspective, the time of the day, and the calmness or agitation of the air. Without hesitation he paints water that contains every hue."

—Theodore Duret

S·E·L·E·C·T·I·N·G
FABRIC

With so many choices of fabric available, it can become rather confusing when you set out to select the fabrics for your landscape. If you enjoy making these kinds of quilts, you will find yourself drawn to batiks, tone-on-tones, and hand-painted and hand-dyed fabrics.

In Creating Your Own Fabric (pages 49–56), we will explore Procion dyeing and fabric painting techniques, giving you the opportunity to create your own unique fabrics. But with so many fabulous commercial fabrics, you can create stunning landscape quilts without getting your hands dirty.

Sky Fabrics

If you can find a fabric with a good range of colors, values, or both, you may well be able to create a beautiful mosaic sky from one piece of fabric. When you plan the tiles (page 58), make sure you include a range of hues from a multicolored fabric. If you are working on a monochromatic sky, you will need a range of values from dark to light.

Here are examples of commercial fabrics that work well. You may not be able to find these exact fabrics, but the photos will give you an idea of what to look for when you are out fabric shopping.

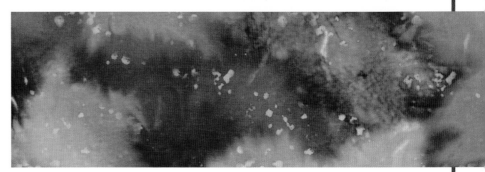
Magical blue fabric with range of values—perfect to create sunny skies

Beautiful multicolored fabric suitable for striking sky

Range of values for cloudy sky—this fabric would also be wonderful to overpaint.

Plainer fabric in beautiful rich colors that harmoniously flow from one to another

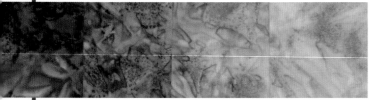

One piece of textured gray batik folded with good range of values

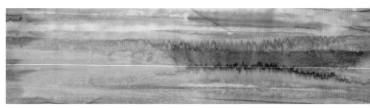

Colorful batik with range of hues

Stormy sky created using gray batik

Beautifully tiled sky created from one fabric by Cathy Lipsen

Don't be dismayed if you can't find the perfect fabric for the sky. You can collect a range of fabrics that blend together to give the effect you are after. It might be a run of orange from light to dark or a run of blue-green to green to yellow-green to yellow. The fabrics can be plain or textured as long as they flow smoothly from one to the next.

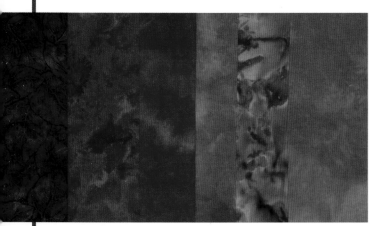

Range of orange fabrics from light to dark

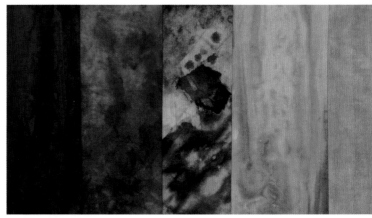

Range of harmonizing colors

Another option is to visit your local home decorator or curtain shop. The fabric samples that include a range of colors are perfect for mosaic tiles. Because the tiles are fused, the fabric doesn't have to be cotton, but take care when ironing.

Range of curtain fabric samples for tiles

Water Fabrics

Keeping in mind that water usually reflects the color of the sky, look for fabrics that remind you of water. Fabric with lines that you can run horizontally will certainly be easily identified as areas of water in your quilt.

Beautiful water fabric with a lot of interest and texture

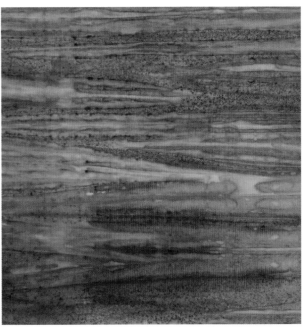

This fabric could be used for land or water.

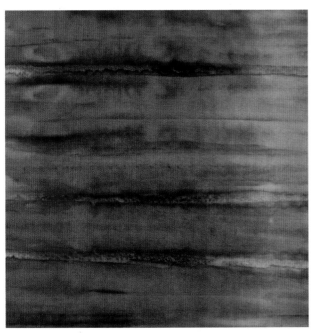

Water reflecting sunrise or sunset

This gorgeous fabric has the feel of water with reflections; it could also be used for land or foliage.

Foliage Fabrics

Of course when I am traveling, I love to visit quilt shops. I am always on the lookout for fabrics for my landscapes, especially batiks that I can cut up and use for foliage. Fabrics that work well are often smaller prints or textures that have light in them. I am not too worried about the pattern, as I will be cutting the fabric pieces small enough that the individual patterns disappear, and I am just left with texture.

Fabrics that work well for foliage

Fabrics for Other Areas

When selecting fabric for hills or other areas more distant in a landscape, avoid those with a distinct pattern. Tone-on-tones, hand-dyes, and subtle textures will work well. Some wonderful textured landscape fabrics are available featuring rocks, grass, tree trunks, and so on. If the scale of the print is appropriate, these can work very well in the foreground. If the color doesn't work, consider overpainting to harmonize with the sky.

C·R·E·A·T·I·N·G
YOUR OWN FABRIC

With so many beautiful commercial fabrics available, why would you ever want to dye your own? Dyeing allows you to create one-of-a-kind fabrics where you control the color, value, and texture. Dyeing fabric is messy, economical, and very exciting. But be careful—it can be addictive!

Dyeing Fabric Using Procion Cold Water Dyes

Procion dyes are very popular with quilters, as they are very colorfast, are easy to use, and have an extensive color range. The colors have different names depending on where you buy them. For example, the same shade of yellow might be called Lemon Yellow by one company, Citrus Yellow by another company, and Yellow MX8G by a third company.

PURCHASING DYES AND CHEMICALS

To get started you need only four colors. I would suggest:

Yellow MX8G	Blue MXG
Red MX8B	Black MX2R

Once you become more comfortable with the process you can add extra colors. The extra dyes I use are:

Yellow MX4G	Rubine MXBA	Lichen MX
Yellow MX3RA	Violet MXRA	Brown MX2R
Orange MX2R	Violet MX2B	Black MXG
Red MXBG	Turquoise MXG	
Magenta MXB	Navy MXGD	

Refer to the color comparison chart (page 50) for equivalent colors by other dye suppliers.

You also need soda ash (sodium carbonate), sometimes called dye activator. In the United States, soda ash is readily available from dye suppliers and many art supply stores (see Resources, page 127). Soda ash can also be purchased at pool supply stores, or you may be able to find it in your supermarket in the laundry detergent section. In Australia it is marketed as Lectric Soda. You also need cooking salt, which can also be purchased in bulk at the supermarket.

The following techniques are those that I currently use for my own pieces. There are a lot of great books on fabric dyeing that will give you many more techniques.

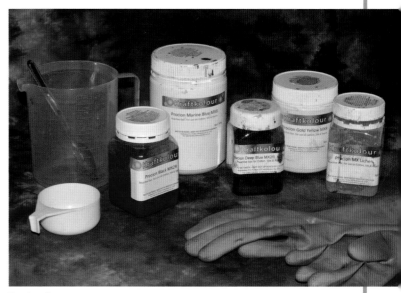

Procion dyes

COLOR COMPARISON CHART

	Kraftkolour	Dharma	Jacquard	PRO Chemical & Dye
Yellow	Yellow MX8G	#1 Lemon Yellow	#004 Lemon Yellow	#1202 Citrus Yellow
	Yellow MX3R	#4 Deep Yellow	#010 Golden Yellow	#104 Golden Yellow
	Yellow MX4G	#2 Bright Yellow		#108 Sun Yellow
Orange	Orange MX2R	#6 Deep Orange	#020 Brilliant Orange	#202 Strong Orange
Red	Red MX8B	#13 Fuchsia	#040 Fuchsia	#308 Fuchsia
	Red MXBG	#10A Chinese Red	#030 Firemen Red	#310 Basic Red
Magenta	Magenta MXB	#65 Raspberry	#042 Raspberry	#335 Berry
Rubine	Rubine MXBA	#16 Maroon	#124 Burgundy	#3208 Maroon
Violet	Violet MXRA	#119 Red Violet	#050 Deep Purple	#801 Grape
	Violet MX2B	#18 Deep Purple	#058 Marine Violet	#810 Blue Violet
Blue	Blue MXG	#23 Cerulean Blue	#070 Cerulean Blue	#406 Intense Blue
Turquoise	Turquoise MXG	#25 Turquoise	#068 Turquoise	#410 Turquoise
Navy	Navy MX4B	#130 Strong Navy	#078 Navy	#412 Navy
Lichen	Lichen MX	#47 Chartreuse	#107 Avocado	#705 Kiwi
Brown	Chocolate MX2B	#35A Chocolate	#119 Chocolate	#511 Chocolate
Black	Black MXG	#39 Black	#150 Jet Black	#602 Cotton Black
	Black MX2R	#44 Better Black	#128 Warm Black	#608 Black

GETTING READY TO DYE

N O T E • • • • • • • • • • • • • • • • • •

Be sure to wear rubber gloves and a dust mask when mixing dyes, and always work in a well-ventilated area.

Fabric

You can use fabric that is 100% cotton, rayon, silk, bamboo, or a blend of these fibers. Cut your fabric into manageable lengths. I usually dye fabric in 1-yard (1-meter) lengths. The first step is to wash the fabric in hot soapy water and rinse well to remove any sizing, finishing, or starch. I use the hot water cycle on my washing machine so that I can be stitching or catching up on a good book while my machine does all the work.

Soda Ash Solution

For the dye to be "fixed," you must create alkaline conditions. In a large container such as a bucket, mix 1 cup of cooking salt and 8 teaspoons of soda ash with some hot water. Stir well until both powders are completely dissolved. Continue adding cold water up to the 2½-gallon (10-liter) mark. This soda ash solution will last up to a week.

Dye Stock

In a glass jar, mix 1 flat tablespoon of dye powder with a small amount of hot water to make a paste. Continue adding cold water in small amounts to make up to 1 cup. Make sure all the powder is completely dissolved. I will refer to this as the dye stock solution. Covered and in the fridge, this solution will keep for a few months.

Now you are ready to have some fun creating spectacular one-of-a-kind fabrics.

THE DYEING PROCESS

Step 1

Swish the prewashed fabric in the bucket of soda ash solution (page 50), wring out the excess moisture, and arrange the fabric in a tray. You can arrange up to 2 yards (2 meters). Empty kitty litter trays, old photo-developing trays, and worn-out baking dishes are all useful receptacles for dyeing.

Step 2

Make up cups of dye in different colors by diluting your dye stock solution (page 50) with water. Your best option for diluting is to pour a small amount of dye stock solution into another jar and add the desired amount of water: add up to a cup of water for paler colors or only a quarter of a cup for deep, rich, intense colors.

Select the combination of colors you want to apply to your fabric. You might like to try an analogous scheme (page 32) or a light-to-dark combination. Or then again, you might just like to experiment using a lot of colors for one piece.

Step 3

Pour the selected colors over different parts of the fabric, using the darker colors sparingly. Mix and press out some of the air bubbles. More movement of the fabric will make a more even color. You can keep the colors separate or blend them completely.

Pour first color (Lichen MX) on fabric arranged in tray.

Add second color (Turquoise MXG).

Add third color (Yellow MX3R).

Step 4

Refer to Washing and Drying Dyed Fabric (page 53).

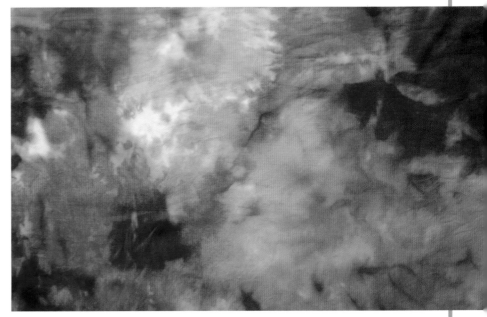

Finished piece

DYEING GRADUATED COLORS

Step 1

Swish the prewashed fabric in the bucket of soda ash solution (page 50), wring out excess moisture, and arrange the fabric in a tray.

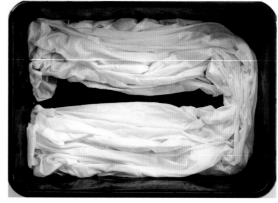

Arrange fabric in tray.

Step 2

Dilute dye stock solution (page 50) with water. Pour the colors over the fabric, starting at one end and overlapping colors as you go. Massage the fabric so that the areas of white disappear.

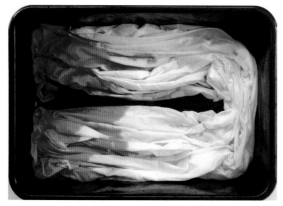

Start with one color (Orange MX2R).

Add second color (Yellow MX4G).

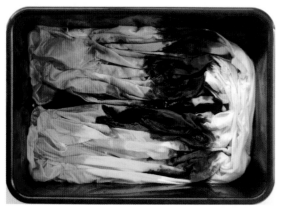

Add third color (Turquoise MXG).

Add last color (Blue MXG).

Step 3

Refer to Washing and Drying Dyed Fabric (page 53).

Finished piece

Dye mop-up fabric and add soda ash solution.

Fabulous result, never to be repeated

DYEING IN LAYERS

A process that I often use if I want to dye pieces that overlap in color is to layer them in a container so the colors blend out from one level to another. This works extremely well if you are dyeing fabric for a colorwash quilt or if you want a range of fabrics that run from dark to light.

Layer 1

Swish 1 yard (1 meter) of prewashed fabric in a bucket of soda ash solution (page 50), wring out the excess moisture, and arrange in the base of a container.

Pour selected colors of diluted dye stock (page 50) over this layer. Massage so that the fabric is almost completely covered in dye. This is usually the darkest layer.

Layer 2

Swish another yard of prewashed fabric in the bucket of soda ash solution, wring out the excess moisture, and arrange in the same container on top of the previous piece. Press down to pick up some of the dye color from the first layer. Add more diluted dye stock solution in a different color or colors or the same color but more diluted. Press down so some of this color passes down to the fabric on the bottom.

Subsequent Layers

Continue in this manner, adding layers of fabric and changing the colors as you go or using more dilute dyes. After you have poured the final dye on your fabric, leave it for at least 24 hours before washing it out. These pieces can all be washed together.

Fabrics dyed in layers in one tray

WASHING AND DRYING DYED FABRIC

Leave the fabric in the trays for at least 24 hours and then pour off any excess dye. Rinse the fabric in cold water first and then, using the hot cycle, wash the fabric in your washing machine. Check the rinse water to make sure it is clear. I usually need to wash the fabric in my top-loading washing machine only once, but if you are using a front-loading machine, you may need to wash it two or three times. Put similar colors together—for example, blues and violets—but avoid washing yellow with other colors if possible. To save energy, hang washed fabric on a line outside or even over furniture near a window to dry. If the weather is not cooperating, dry in your clothes dryer. Iron and fold. This is guaranteed to be the most enjoyable ironing you have ever done.

Dyes used: Yellow MX8G, Orange MX2R, Red MXBG, Black MX2R

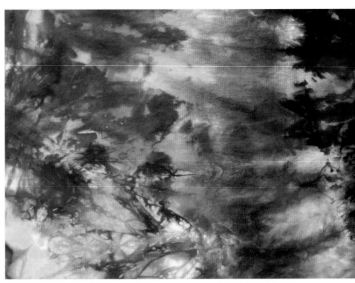

Dyes used: Yellow MX8G, Black MX2R

Dyes used: Yellow MX8G, Yellow MX4G, Black MX2R

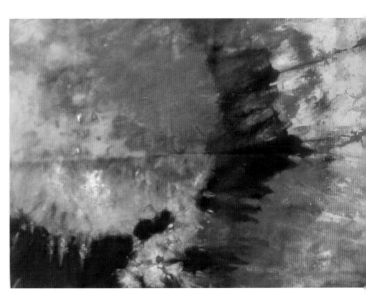

Dyes used: Red MX8B, Blue MWG, Yellow MX3RA

Dyes used: Yellow MX4G, Yellow MX3R, Violet MXG

Dyes used: Yellow MX3RA, Orange MX2R, Black MX2R

Painting Fabric

Another way of creating your own fabric is to use fabric paint. This is quicker, less messy, and, in many ways, more manageable than dyeing fabric. I have been known to paint fabric at 4 a.m. when I can't find the right color in my stash. The colors attained will be less intense and show less depth than the colors in hand-dyed fabric. You do have more control over the color and value, though, and you can create beautiful skies, fabulous water, and stunning trees.

There are quite a few different fabric paints on the market, and I have provided information on some brands and availability in Resources (page 127).

PAINTING SKIES

The secret of painting sky fabric is to start with some simple skies and gradually work your way up to the more dramatic ones.

1. Dilute the paint, mixing approximately 2 or 3 parts water to 1 part paint. This will vary, of course, depending on the depth or darkness of the color you want to use.

2. Moisten the fabric by spraying it or submerging it in a container of water. Stretch the fabric onto a solid, nonporous surface, easing out any air bubbles and removing loose threads. Melamine boards, available from hardware shops, are perfect and can be easily cleaned.

3. Apply the diluted color with foam brushes or sponges. Dabbing creates texture, while long strokes produce smooth color. Begin with the lightest colors first, laying down a basic wash of paint and blending the colors. Most people find it easier to paint from the horizon upward. You can always go darker, but sometimes it is difficult to go lighter. Then it is time to go back over areas, creating highlights and contrasts.

Begin with lightest colors, laying down basic wash.

Add more intense color.

Go back over areas, creating highlights.

4. When you have finished painting, place the fabric, still stretched on the board, in the sun to dry. If it is 4 a.m., you can dry the fabric with a hair dryer, being careful not to wake up the rest of the family.

5. After the fabric is dry, remove it from its base and iron for 2 minutes on the reverse side. Try to allow at least 48 hours after ironing before washing by hand in warm water. Allow the washed fabric to dry and then press it for use.

Sky fabrics ready to be used as one piece or cut up

PAINTING WATER

It is important at all times to reinforce the impression that water is horizontal. Even when the water is broken by waves, it is still basically a flat plane. Lines or elements that make the water look like it is going uphill must be avoided at all costs. Use a large brush and apply horizontal brushstrokes.

Start with plain white cotton fabric or a commercial fabric with a subdued horizontal pattern.

Painting over commercial fabric with horizontal lines

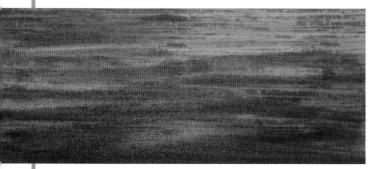

Finished fabric, ironed and ready to use

PAINTING FOLIAGE

Use a combination of painting and sponging to create interesting textures and color combinations that can be cut up for foliage.

Shades of yellow, orange, and blue applied with foam brush

Shades of yellow, orange, and blue applied with sponge to create texture

C·O·N·S·T·R·U·C·T·I·N·G
THE BACKGROUND

Drawing the Design

After you have worked through the design process and guidelines as outlined in Designing Your Quilt (pages 8–21), it is time to make a full-size drawing of the background. At this stage, concentrate on simplifying the background into the main areas, keeping in mind perspective and the position of the horizon line. Sometimes it can be helpful to try to visualize the scene in three to five big shapes, looking past the detail that you add later.

Initial photo taken in Namibia

1. Draw the background and then number the segments from the back of the scene to the front. If there are areas to be fused in place on the background, mark these also— these will be areas that are very small or have an irregular edge. It is preferable to turn under the top edge on the larger pieces, as this technique gives more perspective.

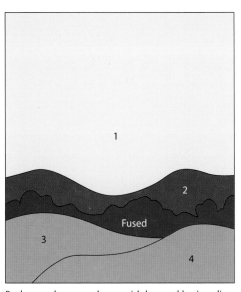

Background pattern drawn with lowered horizon line

2. Place a sheet of freezer paper, shiny side down, onto the pattern. Trace the background segments onto the dull side of the freezer paper. Make sure to include the number of each segment. Cut out each freezer-paper segment separately. Trace Segment 2 to include the fused area.

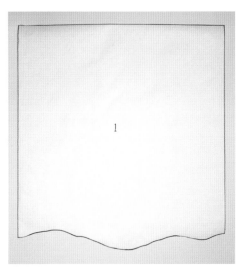

Freezer-paper pattern for sky segment

Choosing Segments to Tile

Now it is time to choose the segment to be tiled. Generally this is one large area, but multiple areas can be tiled, as discussed in Using Tiles in Other Areas (pages 75–84).

After reading the information on tile shapes (pages 20 and 21), choose the shape and size of the background tiles. Squares, rectangles, and diamonds are good options to get you started. Select the fabrics for the mosaic tile shapes. The selection can include a number of different fabrics or one fabric with interesting changes in color.

Group of fabrics for sky

Single piece of fabric with variation in color

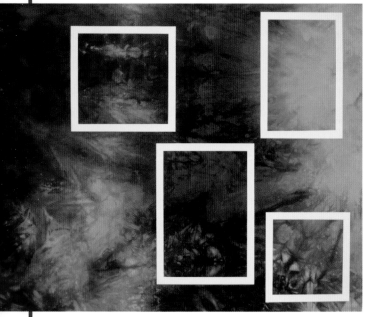

Select different areas of color for tiles.

Making the Tiles

If you are using multiple fabrics, iron a piece of fusible web to the back of each one, following the manufacturer's instructions. If you are using a multicolored fabric, you need to decide which areas you will use for the tiles and iron fusible web to those portions. You will need to feature the different colors, but you will also need areas that show the change from one color to another. These areas become the bridges that allow you to make a smooth transition from one color to the next.

When choosing fusible web, Lite Steam-A-Seam 2, which allows the mosaic pieces to adhere to the background before ironing, is a good choice (see Tip below).

TIP •

Lite Steam-A-Seam 2 is often sold on a roll, so your first step is to cut it into manageable rectangles approximately 6″ × 8″ (15cm × 20cm). This product is also available precut to this size. It has lining paper on both sides, so the roll doesn't stick together. You need to remove the lining paper from one side and then iron the glue side to the back of your fabric. You can use this product with or without steam, and you should set your iron temperature according to the type of fabric you are using, following the manufacturer's instructions. Leaving the backing paper still attached, rotary cut the fabric backed with fusible web into the selected shapes.

CUTTING RECTANGULAR TILES

Rectangular tiles can be cut to any size, but a suggestion is to rotary cut fabric backed with fusible web into strips ¾" (2cm) wide and then cut across the strips every 2" (5cm) to form ¾" × 2" (2cm × 5cm) rectangles. The size of the tiles will depend on the size of the quilt and the area to be tiled. For small quilts, the tile size can be reduced, but take care you don't make them too small, as arranging them symmetrically can be very time consuming.

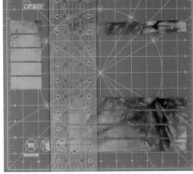

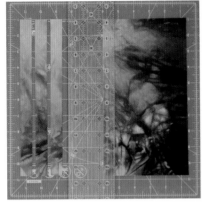

Cut strips.

Crosscut to form rectangles.

Arrange rectangles in piles according to color.

If there is a defined line in your fabric, you will need to make a decision as to which way you cut the fabric. You will get very different effects depending on your decision. Generally, it works well to run the line along the length of the rectangles rather than the width.

Fabric with defined line

Strips cut along length of pattern

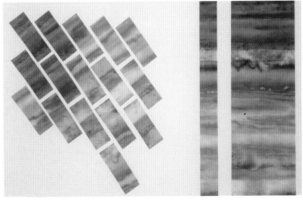

Strips cut across pattern

CUTTING SQUARE TILES

Square tiles can also be cut to any size, but I would suggest that 1½" × 1½" (3.8cm × 3.8cm) to 2" × 2" (5cm × 5cm) is a good size to work with, as the colors and fabrics blend well when the tiles are not too large. Follow the manufacturer's instructions to add fusible web to the selected fabric back. Then rotary cut the fabric into strips of your chosen width. Crosscut at the same width to make squares.

Cut strips.

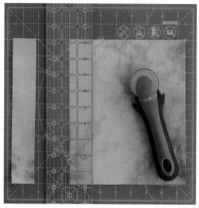

Crosscut to form squares.

If the fabric has a horizontal pattern, you will need to cut the squares on the bias so that you don't have lines heading off in all directions in the mosaic background.

Line up 45° line of ruler with straight edge of fabric and cut along edge of ruler.

Rotary cut parallel strips at selected width.

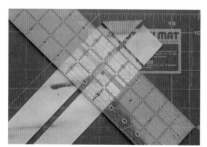

Crosscut to form squares with consistent lines.

TIP • • • • • • • • • • •

A cutting mat that rotates can be very useful for cutting squares and rectangles. You don't need to move your fabric to cut in the other direction—you just rotate the board.

CUTTING DIAMOND TILES

For some, cutting accurate diamond tiles can be a challenge. I have found the following technique a helpful one for my students to follow.

1. Cut a sheet of fusible web and check to see which side of the lining paper has the web attached. You can do this by peeling apart a corner. Leaving both pieces of the paper liner in position, draw a straight line ½" (1.3cm) in from the bottom edge, making sure you draw on the side that has the web attached. Position a ruler so the 30° line is on the drawn line. Draw a second line along the edge of the ruler.

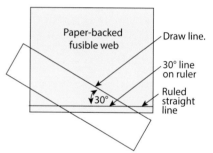

Draw 30° line on fusible web.

2. Turn over the ruler to the back and position the same 30° line along the initial dawn line. Draw a third line along the edge of the ruler.

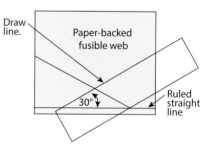

Turn ruler over and draw another 30° line.

3. Choose the width of the tiles, considering 1"–2" (2.5cm–5cm) as a suitable size. Most of the diamond tiles featured in the quilts in this book have been cut at 1½" (3.8cm). Draw lines at a chosen width, parallel to the second and third lines, until the whole grid is filled in.

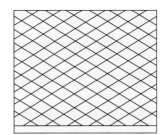

Draw parallel lines at chosen width until grid is covered.

4. Follow the manufacturer's instructions to iron the fusible web to the back of the selected fabric or fabrics. Following the grid, cut out the diamond shapes with a rotary cutter or scissors.

If you are using multiple fabrics, the grid can be cut up and sections ironed to the back of different fabrics.

This technique allows you to position the fusible web grid so that any lines in the fabric can be aligned with the longest part of the diamond.

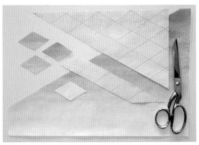

Cut diamonds using grid as guide.

Cut grid into sections and fuse to back of different fabrics.

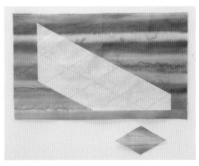

Position diamonds along linear pattern on fabric.

Alternative Techniques for Cutting Diamond Tiles

An alternative to drawing the grid on fusible web is to trace around individual diamond stencils, which are available in multiple sizes. These are very useful if you are just cutting one or two shapes from many different fabrics. Trace the diamonds onto fusible web and cut out the shape with a ¼" (6mm) margin. Follow the manufacturer's instructions to fuse these diamonds to the back of the fabrics and cut out along the drawn lines. For this process you can use scissors or a small rotary cutter.

The following is another alternative that works well for those who are not "spatially challenged."

1. Apply the fusible web to the back of the fabrics, following the manufacturer's instructions.

2. Choose the width of the diamond, for example, 1½" (3.8cm), and cut multiple strips this width.

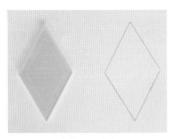

Trace around diamond shape on fusible web.

Cut out with ¼" (6mm) margin, fuse to back of fabric, and cut out.

Cut strips.

3. Find the 60° line on the ruler and position this on the top edge of the strip. Rotary cut at a 60° angle across the end of the strip.

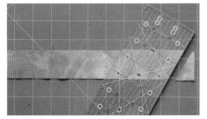

Position 60° line on top edge of fabric strip and cut 60° angle at strip end.

4. Now from each strip, move the ruler to cut multiple diamonds that measure 1½″ (3.8cm).

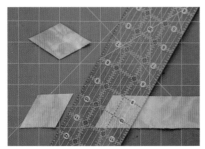

Cut across at 1½″ (3.8cm).

TIP • • • • • • • • • • •
Be careful when cutting fabric with a linear pattern if you are using this technique. You don't want lines heading off in all directions.

Choosing the Base Fabric

The next step is to choose a base fabric to go under the tiles. A fabric that blends and is of a middle value is often the best choice. To select this fabric, look at your color range and choose a color that is in the middle. Then look at the value. You don't want a fabric that is too light or dark; one that has a middle value, taking into consideration your other fabrics, should work well. Try placing some tiles on a number of different base fabrics to see the effect.

Base color that blends and is of middle value

Base that is similar color but lighter value

Alternatively, a contrasting fabric can work well, depending on your design. On occasion I have used the same multicolored fabric for the tiles and the base, which allows for contrast in some areas and more harmony in others.

Don't rush this part of the process. Try as many options as you can. Stand back and squint to see which one you like best and which one gives you the desired effect. After you have selected the base fabric, iron the freezer-paper pattern for the tiled segment onto the right side of the selected background fabric. Cut out the fabric with a generous 1" (2.5cm) seam allowance around the outside of the freezer paper. Then remove the freezer paper.

Tiles on contrasting base

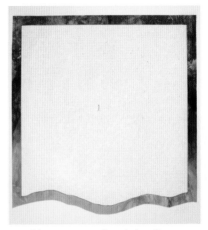

Base fabric cut out and ready for tiling

TIP • • • • • • • • • • •

If the freezer paper is too narrow, you can join sheets by overlapping the sides and ironing them together. Or you can tape them together using masking tape on the dull side of the freezer paper.

Tiles on same multicolored fabric

Placing the Tiles

It is now time to position the tiles on the background. Have fun! It feels like painting by numbers!

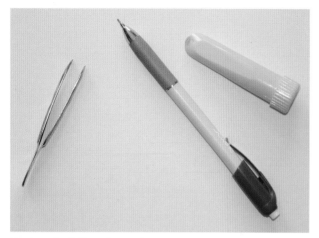

Handy tools: chalk markers and tweezers

RECTANGULAR TILES IN THE SKY

1. Your first decision is to determine the angle that you will use for the placement of the rectangles. It can be quite steep or a much gentler slope. A 45° angle is a popular choice, but it depends on your design. It can be a slope, as illustrated below, or any other angle you choose.

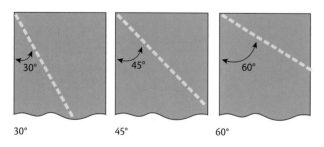

30°   45°   60°

2. Position a rotary cutting ruler at your chosen angle and draw a line in chalk or marking pencil along the edge. Draw additional guidelines parallel to the first line and about 3″ (8cm) apart.

Base fabric with guidelines

3. With the lining paper of the fusible web still attached to the tiles, arrange the tiles along the edge of the line. Start ½″ (1.3cm) from the edge and leave a small space, approximately ³⁄₁₆″ (5mm), between the tiles. Keeping in mind your color selection, try to incorporate gradual color changes. Continue placing the tiles down to ½″ (1.3cm) from the bottom edge of the segment.

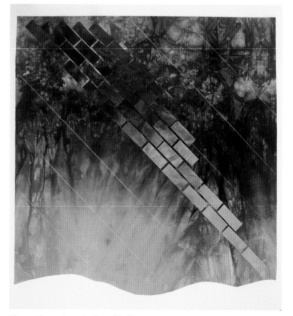

Place tiles using chalk guidelines.

To help you estimate the gap between the tiles, keep in mind that ³⁄₁₆″ (5mm) is just bigger than ⅛″ (3mm) but smaller than ¼″ (6mm).

4. Continue adding rows of tiles parallel to the first, but position each tile as if you were building a brick wall, with the rows approximately ³⁄₁₆″ (5mm) apart. Alternatively, place each additional row of tiles a third of the way down the previous tile row to disguise the brick wall effect.

Brick wall placement

Tiles positioned one-third down

TIP •

Don't be too fussy about accuracy at this stage, as you will have the chance to line up the tiles accurately in Step 5.

5. Continue placing tiles until the sky background segment is covered. Peel the lining paper from each rectangle and carefully and accurately position the tiles until you are happy with the arrangement. The adhesive on the fusible web will allow each tile to adhere in place, but if on reflection you change your mind, it can be carefully lifted and replaced by another tile. Tweezers are very useful for this part of the process.

6. Pin the sky to your design wall and stand back. If you are happy with the positioning of the colors, the value changes, and the accuracy of the placement, iron to fuse the tiles permanently to their base.

Finished tiled base

TIP • • • • • • • • • •
Use a pressing sheet over the tiles when ironing them to the base. Press for 6–15 seconds with a hot iron for cotton fabric. Repeat the process, overlapping pressed areas.

SQUARE TILES IN THE SKY

1. Choose the base fabric for the sky. Position a rotary cutting ruler with the 45° line along the right side edge of the base fabric. Draw a line on the base fabric in chalk or marking pen. Draw a series of lines approximately 3″ (8cm) apart parallel to this line.

Reposition the ruler at 45° to the left side of the base fabric and draw a line. Draw more parallel lines, as outlined as in Step 3 (top of page 61).

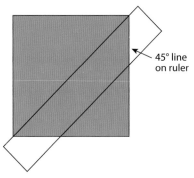

45° line on ruler

Place 45° line on ruler along right edge.

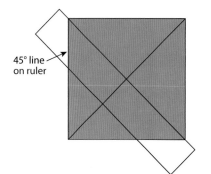

45° line on ruler

Place 45° line on ruler along left edge.

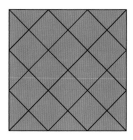

2. Position the tiles along the edge of the line, starting ½″ (1.3cm) from the top corner. Leave a small space, approximately 3⁄16″ (5mm), between the tiles. Keep in mind your color selection and try to create gradual color changes. Continue placing the tiles down to the bottom edge of the segment.

Begin placing tiles in position using marked guidelines.

3. Continue to add more tiles, keeping the spaces even between the squares, until the base fabric is covered.

4. When you are happy with the placement, peel the lining paper from each square and place the tiles carefully and accurately in position. The adhesive on the fusible web will allow each tile to adhere in place. But if on reflection you change your mind, it can be carefully lifted with tweezers and replaced by another tile.

Pin the sky to your design wall and stand back. If you are happy with the placement of the tiles, iron to fuse the tiles permanently to their base.

Base covered in tiles

DIAMONDS IN THE SKY

1. Position a rotary cutting ruler with the 60° line along the right side edge of the sky base fabric. Draw a line on the base fabric in chalk or marking pen.

Reposition the ruler at 60° to the left side of the base fabric and draw a line. Draw a series of lines approximately 3″ apart and parallel to these lines to create a grid.

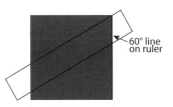

Place 60° line on ruler along right edge.

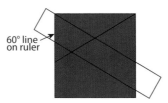

Place 60° line on ruler along left edge.

Draw additional parallel lines.

2. Position the tiles along the edge of the line, starting ½″ (1.3cm) from the top corner. Leave a small space, approximately ³⁄₁₆″ (5mm), between the tiles. Keep in mind your color selection and try to create gradual changes. Continue placing the tiles down to the bottom edge of the segment.

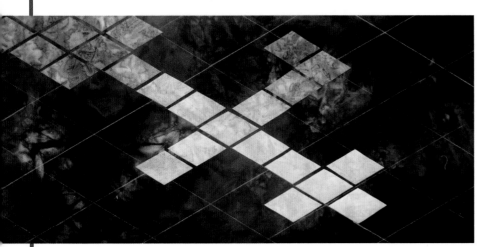

Begin placing tiles in position using marked guidelines.

3. Continue to add more tiles, keeping the spaces even between the diamonds, until the background is covered.

4. When you are satisfied with the placement, peel the lining paper from each diamond and position the tiles in place. The adhesive on the fusible web will allow each tile to adhere in place. But if on reflection you change your mind, it can still be carefully lifted with tweezers and replaced by another tile.

5. Pin the base to your design wall to check the placement of the tiles. If you are happy with the placement, iron to fuse the tiles permanently to their base.

Continue adding tiles until base is covered.

Stitching Down the Tiles

Before the tiles are stitched down, the base is placed in position on the batting and quilt backing fabric. The stitching is part of the quilting process, as you will stitch through several layers.

BATTING

There are a number of excellent battings on the market today, including wool, cotton, bamboo, polyester, rayon, and silk. Any of these products would be suitable as long as the batting is not too thick and bulky.

QUILT BACKING

The choice of backing fabric for the quilt is up to you, but there are a few things to keep in mind. Use a commercial or hand-dyed fabric that does not have a high thread count, as this will be easier for quilting. Fabrics such as batiks do have a very high thread count and can make the quilting process more difficult. Even with a walking foot, batiks, when used as backings, tend to drag, creating tucks. The needle struggles sometimes to stitch cleanly through all the layers (keep in mind that the top layer is a tile backed with fusible web).

The color of the backing fabric is also a personal choice, but I do like to match the backing fabric to the color of the quilt top.

MAKING THE QUILT SANDWICH

The size for the quilt backing and batting will be determined by the way you want to finish your quilt. The Finishing Techniques section (page 99) discusses three different techniques to complete your quilt. The technique that you will use will determine the size to cut the backing and batting. For example, if you want to use the Making a Faced edge technique, you would cut the backing and batting at least 2" (5cm) larger than the dimensions of the quilt top. If your quilt top is 12" × 18" (31cm × 46cm), then cut the backing and batting at least 14" × 20" (36cm × 51cm). However, if you want to add borders to the quilt center, you will need to cut the backing and batting larger still, taking into account the desired size of the borders. For example, to add a 4" (10cm) border, add an extra 9" (23cm). The batting is cut the same size as the backing, so align the batting with the backing. Then position the sky section on top of the batting in at least 4" from the top and both sides to allow for the planned 4" border. Pin the layers together using safety pins or straight pins.

Cut batting and backing fabric larger than quilt top.

THREADS FOR STITCHING TILES

The choice of the color and type of thread for stitching down the tiles is crucial. Unwind some thread and place it across the tiles to see which works best. Generally, you are looking for the thread that is the least obvious or evident. For most designs, you don't want the stitching on the tiles to be a distraction in the background.

Match thread to tile color.

Choosing Thread Type

For the top thread, I have found that rayon, silk, or polyester thread works well. This appears to create a softer, subtler line across the tiles, compared to the bolder and at times harsh line created by cotton thread. The thread should be a 40-weight or finer.

I generally match the weight of the bobbin thread to the top thread and choose a color that blends. I match the bobbin thread color to the top thread rather than matching it to the color of the backing fabric.

Choosing Thread Color

I have found that variegated threads generally give better results than plain colors. In the past, variegated threads were quite difficult to use, as the run of each color seemed endless and the color combination left a bit to be desired. Now many of the variegated threads change color every inch and the color combinations are superb. If the background tiles range from violet to red to orange, then a variegated thread in these colors will work well. Even though there will be touches of violet thread on the orange tiles and vice versa, the traces of these colors provide gentle highlights and harmony across the surface. If you can't find a variegated thread that blends with your tiles, a plain thread in the middle color and value is your best option. When searching for this thread, keep in mind that it may be a very similar color to your base fabric.

NEEDLES

The choice of sewing machine needle is also important. Match the needle size to the top thread size. If your thread is 40-weight, then a size 12/80 needle would be a good choice. A 50-weight thread would require a 10/70 needle. I use top-stitch needles for quilting, as they allow the thread to pass through the layers easily, without breaking. Check your thread manufacturer's website for a guide to needle sizes, as there are some variations.

STITCHING

As you are stitching down the tiles, you are actually quilting through the sandwich, stitching through many layers. If you have a walking foot, it will make the job much easier.

TIP • • • • • • • • • • • •
If your walking foot allows you an open-toe view, then you can be even more accurate. Check to see whether this option is available.

Open-toe walking foot

Top Tension

Make up a practice sandwich so that you can check your machine's tension before you start quilting the tiled area. If you can see the bobbin thread coming through to the top, you need to loosen the top tension. If you usually sew with a tension of 4, you would need to lower this to 3 or 2. Keep lowering the tension until you can't see the bobbin thread on the top. If you find that the bobbin thread is too tight underneath and the top thread is loose, you need to tighten the top tension. Move it from 4 to 5 and then check to see whether you have complete, properly formed stitches on the top and the bottom.

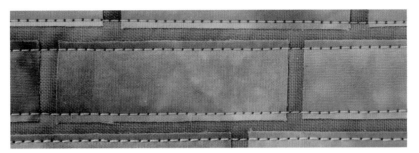

Quilt top—top tension too high in top rows

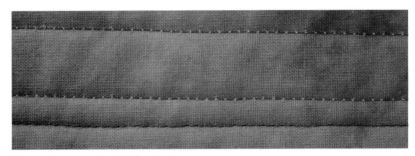

Quilt back—top tension too low in top row

STITCHING RECTANGLES

Begin at the top corner, stitching approximately ⅛" (3mm) in from the edges of the tiles, and continue down to the bottom of each row. Pass along the bottom and then stitch back up along the other side of the tiles. You don't need to stitch across the narrow end of the tiles. Continue until all the tiles are stitched down.

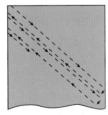

Direction of stitching

Match thread to tile color

STITCHING SQUARES AND DIAMONDS

1. Begin at the top corner, stitching approximately ⅛″ (3mm) in from the edges of the tiles, and continue down to the bottom of each row. Turn and come back up on the opposite side of the tile. Continue until all the tiles are stitched on 2 sides.

2. After you have stitched down 2 sides, begin the process again from the opposite top corner. Continue until all 4 sides are stitched.

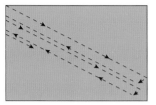

Direction of stitching

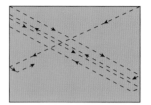

Repeat process on opposite side.

Stitching Down the Rest of the Background

After you have quilted the top section, it is time to add the other background segments.

These segments may be appliquéd or fused in position.

First audition the foreground fabrics. Fold fabrics in position and stand back to see whether the colors are in harmony with the tiled sky and provide some perspective (see Color and Perspective, pages 43 and 44).

Audition foreground fabrics

APPLIQUÉD SEGMENTS

1. After you have selected the fabrics, press the appropriate freezer-paper segments to the right side of your chosen fabrics. Cut out the fabric sections with a ½″ (1.3cm) seam allowance around each segment.

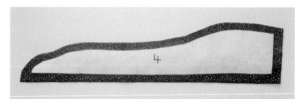

Cut out with ½″ (1.3cm) seam allowance.

2. Trim the top edge of each fabric segment to ¼″ (6mm) and clip the curves. Press the seam allowance to the back. It is easier to do this with the freezer paper still in position.

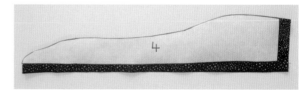

Trim top edge and press to back.

3. Remove the freezer paper and position the segment in place on the quilt sandwich. Pin the segment in position, pinning at right angles to the seam.

Segment 2 pinned in position.

4. Stitch down the segments using the invisible appliqué stitch on your sewing machine.

Invisible Appliqué

GETTING READY TO STITCH

Because you will be stitching through the segment, the batting, and the backing, use your walking foot. Thread the top of your machine with a good-quality invisible thread such as Monopoly, made by Superior Threads, or Wonder Thread, made by YLI. Fill the bobbin with a thread that matches the backing fabric color. Insert a fine needle, such as the size 8/60 microtex/sharp, and attach the walking foot. Select the blind hem or appliqué stitch from the stitch menu.

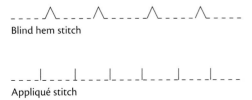

Blind hem stitch

Appliqué stitch

The settings for the invisible blind hem stitch will vary depending on the brand of your machine. For Bernina, most Pfaff, and Janome machines, reduce the stitch width to a little narrower than 1. It should be just wide enough to barely catch two or three threads of the top fabric. Also adjust the stitch length to a little under 1. The zigzag stitches should be ⅛"–¼" (3mm–6mm) apart. The setting for most Viking/Husqvarna machines is stitch length 0.3 and stitch width 1.0. When considering your options, the stitch that is the most invisible is your first choice.

The tension will probably need to be adjusted because of the very short stitch length being used. Begin by reducing the top tension slightly—that is, turning the top tension dial to one number lower than normal. On a Bernina, thread the bobbin thread through the finger on the bobbin casing to tighten up the bobbin tension.

Check your settings on a sample placed on tear-away stabilizer. Only the zigzag stitch will bite into the top layer. If you see any of the bobbin thread coming through to the top, you need to decrease the top tension further. If you have reduced the top tension all the way down and can still see the bobbin thread on the top, then it is time to take out the bobbin case and tighten the tiny screw on the side. Turn the screw to the right the equivalent distance of 10 minutes on the clock. Replace it in your machine and try again. If you are using a finer bobbin thread than normal, it is a good idea to tighten the bobbin case at the beginning.

Adjusting bobbin tension

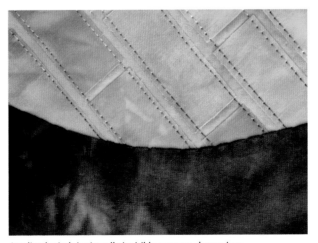

Appliqué stitch is virtually invisible even on closer view.

APPLIQUÉING SEGMENTS

1. When you are happy with the invisible appliqué stitches on a practice sample, sew along the pressed-under edge of Segment 2, with the zigzag stitch just catching the edge of the Segment 2 fabric and the straight stitches sitting on Segment 1. Because these segments are pinned to the batting and backing, you are stitching through this base as well.

2. Once a segment is stitched in position, if a segment is to be fused, do this before adding subsequent segments. Change the bobbin thread to match the background fabric as necessary to ensure that the stitches are invisible.

FUSED SEGMENTS

If some of the background segments are to be fused in position, they will need to be added in order.

1. Follow the manufacturer's instructions to trace the segments from the *back* of your pattern. Tracing from the back avoids a mirror image of the pattern. If you have a lightbox available, this will make the process much easier.

2. Cut out each segment of fusible web with a generous ¼″ (6mm) margin around the outside.

3. Iron the fusible web to the back of the selected fabric. Cut out along the top drawn line, but leave the extra margin in place on the side and bottom edges. This will become a seam allowance that will be covered by the next segment or border.

Back of segment with seam allowance

Front of segment

4. Press the fused segment in position.

Press fused segment in position.

5. Continue to add the additional fused and appliquéd segments in order until all the background areas are covered as planned in your pattern.

Add segments in order.

Quilting the Landscape Details

After you have all the background segments in position, it is time to quilt the rest of the background, since the tiled sky area is already quilted.

Stitch close to the edge of any fused sections in a matching thread. Add quilting lines to other areas, following the contours of the land or creating your own textures in thread. Free-motion quilting with a darning foot will give more texture to the fabric surface. Think about the textures of tree bark, rippling water, rolling hills, and leaf details. Put those lines into your landscape as you scribble or doodle in thread.

U·S·I·N·G
TILES IN OTHER AREAS

Tiles can give wonderful movement and interest to large areas of sky, but they can be used very effectively in other areas as well. Forests, lakes, mountains, and buildings can also be tiled to create something unique and special.

Forests

After hiking though stunning stands of trees, we are sometimes drawn to re-create these special areas in fabric. A world without trees is unbearable to imagine. They are the earth's oldest and largest living things. Their unique shapes have been the inspiration for artists over the centuries. They can be majestic, at times astonishing, diverse, and utterly captivating. Many of us have a bond with nature and are concerned about the environment. We look for ways to communicate how special trees are. We can photograph them, we can paint them, or we can write poems or text about them. As quilters, we are drawn to use trees as inspiration, detailing their amazing shapes and textures in fabric and thread.

A forest is sometimes filled with the play of light as the sun filters through to some areas and leaves others in mysterious gloomy shade. A way of re-creating this dappled sunshine back-drop is to tile the background in a variety of colors. Highlighting areas of purer colors offset with darker tones, especially toward the base of the forest, can be a very effective setting. The addition of detailed trees and leaves in the foreground will be covered in Foreground Highlights (pages 85–98).

Sunlight shining through forest (Yosemite National Park, California)

MAKING A FOREST BACKGROUND

1. To create a forest backdrop, choose a multicolored fabric or a range of fabrics that mimic the colors in the background of the forest. Consider the season, as this will be an important design element. The colors could range from the stunning autumn tones of reds, browns, oranges, and golds to the new crisp greens of spring, or the gray and white tones of the stark, bleak winter. You can use a collection of fabrics, one multicolored commercial fabric, or even dye your own (see Creating Your Own Fabric, pages 49–56).

Autumn tones

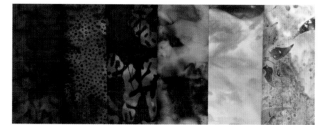
Spring greens

Suitable hand-dyed fabric

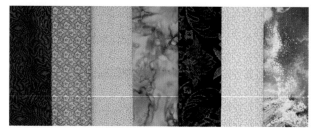
Winter collection

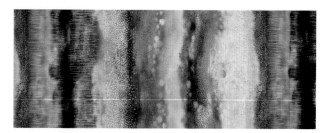
Commercial fabric with winter tones

Commercial fabric with green tones

2. Determine the size of the finished quilt and the format. The very nature of trees is that they are tall and not very wide, so the vertical format is often the most appropriate.

3. Determine the tile shape. Rectangular tiles work well for a forest background, although other shapes can also be effective, depending on the type of forest. Following the instructions in Constructing the Background (pages 57–74), cut the tiles from the various fabrics you have selected. Tiles cut ¾″ × 2¼″ (2cm × 6cm) work well. Remember that the tile size needs to be in proportion to the area you are covering. Make sure you include different values as well as some brighter colors to add highlights.

Background of floral squares with tiles cut 1½″ × 1½″ (3.8cm × 3.8cm)

Tiled section of *Fern Pool* with tiles cut ¾″ × 2¼″ (2cm × 6cm) (full quilt on page 4)

Backdrop of diamond-shaped tiles with tiles cut 1½″ × 1½″ (3.8cm × 3.8cm)

4. Choose the base fabric. Try arranging some of the tiles on a range of possible base fabrics. After you have made your selection, cut the base fabric 2″ larger all around than the planned finished size. You don't need to draw up a pattern at this stage, although you will need to draw the trees full-size later in the process.

5. Decide on the angle of the placement of the tiles. They can be placed vertically or on an angle, depending on the feeling you want to create or on the nature of the forest itself.

Tiles placed on angle

Center Stage by Carol Newhart, 23″ × 34″ (59cm × 89cm)

Tiles placed vertically

Alberta in the Fall by Wendy Greber, 20″ × 34″ (51cm × 86cm)

6. Use a chalk marker or fabric pencil to rule some lines on the base fabric as a guide for tile placement (page 64). For *Fern Pool* (page 4), the guidelines were drawn vertically.

7. Arrange the tiles on the base. I find it helpful to decide on the placement of the highlights first. At this stage, the tiles are still backed with paper, so you can easily move them from one position to another.

8. Add more tiles until the whole forest base is covered.

Arrange highlight tiles first.

Add tiles until base is covered.

9. Remove the paper and fuse the tiles in place permanently.

10. Refer to Constructing the Background (pages 57–74) to layer and stitch the forest background.

Close-up of quilting showing change of thread color to match tiles

Waterways

Capturing water in fabric can be quite a challenge. Water is completely colorless, taking its appearance from the sky, the weather, and the lighting conditions. Lines in the water tend to be horizontal, so placing tiles in a horizontal formation will aid the viewer in recognizing areas of water in your work. Rectangular tiles are an obvious choice for water, but diamonds, placed horizontally, can also be used effectively.

A body of water might be the backdrop of your quilt, or it could be a feature in a smaller area of your design.

To help create perspective, consider reducing the width of rectangular tiles as they recede toward the back of the design.

Horizontal tiles in the foreground can be ⅞″ (2.2cm) wide, then reduce by ⅛″(3mm) to ¾″(2cm), then to ⅝″ (1.6cm), gradually working down to as narrow as ⅜″ (1cm). The length of the tiles can be consistent or varied.

Autumn Reflections by Gloria Loughman, 47″ × 34″ (119cm × 86cm)

Tiles in water show reduction in width and color.

These tiles show reduction in width and length.

Remember that you will also need to graduate the colors for the tiles as they recede toward the back of the design. The tile color will become paler and the pattern less defined. A sunset sky will also have an impact on your color choice, as the glow of the sky will be reflected as a mirror image in the water.

There are quite a few options for tile placement; three are illustrated below.

Bricks

Tiles offset

Random placement, taking into account reflections

REFLECTIONS

As currents and breezes play across the water, reflections are often viewed as a series of horizontal lines on the surface. They are narrow in the distance and gradually become broader in the foreground. Changing the color of the tiles for these areas can be particularly effective. Generally, the shape of the

reflection will be a mirror image of the original, but as the wind picks up and blows across the surface, the shapes—especially thin, narrow lines—can become distorted. These can be easier to manage as stitching later in the process.

Distorted grass (photograph)

Reflection from *Autumn Reflections* (full quilt on previous page)

MAKING A BODY OF WATER

1. Draw out a full-size pattern (see Drawing the Design, page 57). Number each background section, starting at the sky and working forward. Decide on areas to be fused and label them accordingly.

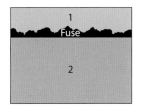

Pattern with numbers included

Okavango Delta, Botswana

2. Trace the main background lines onto the dull side of freezer paper. Trace Segment 1 to include the fused segment. Cut out each individual background segment.

3. Now it is time to make a decision about your color scheme. The water will need to be in harmony with the sky. Collect the fabrics for the water and consider your options for the sky fabric, keeping in mind that the sky needs to be lighter than the water color. You can use a commercial fabric or paint a sky (page 55).

4. Iron the freezer-paper pattern for the sky to the right side of the sky fabric. Cut it out with a ½˝ (1.3cm) seam allowance around the outside.

5. Cut out tiles (page 59). Rectangles placed horizontally will certainly create a water effect. Diamonds positioned horizontally can also be very effective.

6. Select the base fabric by auditioning the tiles on a range of fabrics. Iron the freezer-paper pattern to the right side of the chosen base fabric and cut it out with a 1˝ (2.5cm) seam allowance around the edge.

Cut out base for water with 1˝ (2.5cm) seam allowance.

7. Trace around the edge of the freezer paper with a chalk pen before removing the paper from the fabric. This will give you an outline of the area to be covered.

8. Place and fuse the tiles in place as described in Constructing the Background (pages 57–74). It is important that your lines don't run downhill, or it will appear that the water is running out the side of your design.

Make sure tiles are horizontal.

9. Use the tiled segment as you would any other appliquéd segment (page 72).

TIP •
The entire background for your quilt might be a large body of water. If this is the case, not all the base needs to be covered by tiles. It can be quite effective to leave some areas clear.

Some areas of base fabric left clear of tiles from *Fern Pool* (full quilt on page 4)

Mountains

If you would like a mountain range or hills to be a feature of your landscape, they can be made more eye-catching and interesting when covered in tiles. For this to work in harmony with the rest of the design, the tiles must cover a substantial area of the background. This is similar to the technique used for creating waterways (pages 80–82).

Maroon Bells by Julia Graves, 28" × 34" (71cm × 86cm)

Follow the same process as creating a waterway, from drawing a full-size pattern of the design (Step 1, page 81) through preparing the segments and making the tiles (Step 9, at left). The size of the tiles needs to be in proportion to the segment. Rectangles, diamonds, and squares could all be appropriate shapes for hills and mountains. For flatter areas, rectangles or diamonds would be the best options.

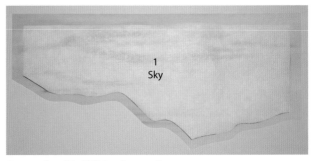

Cut out sky with ½" (1.3cm) seam allowance.

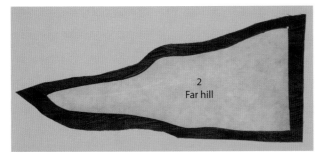

Hill 2 with freezer paper still attached

Tiled hills

With a suitable thread, stitch the tiles in place on the background. It might be helpful to place the segment on a tear-away base to make the stitching easier to manage.

Stitch along edge of tiles.

Use as you would any other appliquéd segment (page 72).

TIP • • • • • • • • • • • • • • • • • •
You can make an overlay of the pattern on tracing paper or clear plastic to place over the top of the sandwich to help you position the segments.

Stitch the segments in place using the invisible appliqué stitch (page 73). Add subsequent segments in order. These segments may be tiled or unadorned and should be stitched in position in the same way.

Tiled Foreground

Some designs have a large area of foreground that can be made more visually exciting with tiles. This works well if the background and middle ground are represented in a more realistic way, allowing you the freedom to apply masses of color and texture to the foreground yet still retain the essence of the original scene.

Follow the instructions in Waterways (pages 80–82) and Mountains (pages 82 and 83) for constructing a quilt with a tiled foreground.

Photo by C&T Publishing

Mountain Meadow by Donna Moog, 36″ × 24″ (91cm × 61cm)

Whole Quilt

If you would like the background to have a more abstract feel, try tiling the whole background. You can incorporate sky, mountains, middle ground, and foreground as you build up your design. Prepare the tiles as described in Constructing the Background (pages 57–74).

It may be helpful to draw a grid of the chosen tile shapes and then outline the various sections of the landscape.

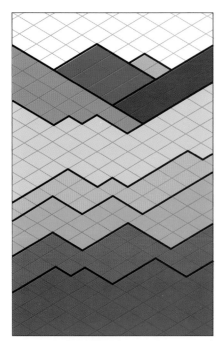

Outline sections on grid.

Choose your base fabric as described in Choosing the Base Fabric (pages 62 and 63); then position the tiles following the pattern on the grid. Work with the lighter-colored tiles in the background, building up to the more saturated colors in the foreground.

Position tiles.

When you are happy with the placement of the tiles, follow the instructions in Stitching Down the Tiles (pages 69–72). You can then add more detail to the surface, such as trees, buildings, or other selected elements. Strong shapes that cross many areas of the quilt will help provide cohesiveness to the design.

Wilkatana by Glenys Elliot, 19″ × 25″ (48cm × 64cm)

Arizona Wildfire by Bonnie L. Pennybacker, 25″ × 18″ (64cm × 46cm)

F·O·R·E·G·R·O·U·N·D
HIGHLIGHTS

After you have quilted the background, it is time to think about the elements you will feature on the surface. Trees with character are an obvious choice, but there are many other shapes that can be used. People, buildings, bridges, and boats work beautifully set against a mosaic sky or water.

Silhouettes

Depending on the time of day, the images might be in silhouette. Silhouettes can be traced back to primitive art forms, as noted in ancient aboriginal rock carvings. They are often very striking images that artists and photographers feature in their landscapes. Silhouettes usually need to be drawn accurately, as they lack other reference points such as texture and color. If your drawing skills still need to improve, it may be helpful to photocopy your photo and enlarge it up to the size you require and then trace the main outline.

NOTE • • • • • • • • • • • • • • • • • •
Remember to follow copyright legislation and photocopy only your own work.

When looking for shapes, try to find those that tell a story. The shapes need to be distinctive and easily recognized.

After the bush fire (Kelowna, Canada)

Author visiting Yosemite National Park, California

Sunset (Savusavu, Fiji)

Vineyard Silhouette by Kerrie Lomman, 18″ × 16″ (46cm × 41cm)

Trees

Trees are so much a part of our everyday scenery that we tend to overlook them and take them for granted. Trees, like people, have distinctive and unique physical characteristics. Some are tall and straight, soaring into the sky, while others are gnarled, bent over, and squat. Their foliage can be a thick blanket of broad leaves, a smattering of fine wispy fronds, or clusters of dangerous, threatening spikes. In late autumn and winter they can be stark naked, and we can really appreciate their beautiful or sometimes ugly forms. Trees are not always stunning and graceful, but you can portray them in a way that can be very appealing to the viewer. If you can capture the personalities of trees, their eccentricities and spirit, you will have achieved a great result—a result that can stir pleasure and excitement in a viewer.

Trees are certainly wonderful elements to include in your artwork. Make an effort to study the trees you see as you travel. See what catches your eye. It may be a color, a shape, or a texture. It may be the relationship between the tree and its setting. It could be the play of light through the leaves or the form of the trunk and the branches.

Photo by Peter McLennam

The Bringer of Light and Fire by Donna Krane, 27″ × 33″ (69cm × 84cm)

Quiver tree (Namibia)

Queensland bottle tree (Australia)

Beautiful color and textures of eucalyptus bark

Towering giant (Yosemite National Park, California)

STYLE

Look through your photos to find a tree that evokes a response. Decide whether you want to make the tree as realistic as possible or follow a more abstract path. You have already made a step down the path toward abstraction by tiling the sky or water. You can go a little further down this track by abstracting the trunks of the trees, stylizing the foliage, or even using geometric shapes for leaves.

Realistic Trees

Drawing trees involves much more than just recording what you see. Try to recognize why a particular tree captures your interest. Think about what elements to include and those that can be left out. Choose shapes, lines, and a color palette that reflect your creative side rather than sticking to the real-life image. You will certainly need to simplify by leaving out unnecessary details, but try to keep the spirit of the tree intact. Your work becomes special because of what you do with your subject matter.

TIP · · · · · · · · · · · · · · · · · · ·
Refer to Designing Your Quilt (pages 8–21) for information about designing and positioning the key elements.

DRAWING TRUNKS

To draw a tree full-size on the pattern, look carefully at the shape of the trunk. Often people think of a trunk as being two parallel lines, and, indeed, there are many trees that fill that brief. But in a composition, a trunk that has character is a much more interesting subject. Just like building a framework of a house, draw the trunk and branches, ignoring the foliage. Like the shingles and roof on a house, the canopy of foliage will be added later. Start drawing the main outline of the trunk and then try adding a few more angles and bends. If appropriate, join the limbs asymmetrically to create individuality, as no two trees are exactly the same.

Think about how the tree is attached to the ground. If there is any kind of aboveground root system, exaggerate it so the tree appears to be attached and growing and not just a piece of fabric fused to the surface of the quilt. If the tree is very close to the foreground of the quilt, consider taking the base of the tree out the bottom of the picture.

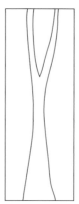
Original drawing

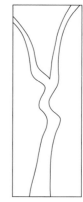
Add more twists for interest.

Symmetrical and asymmetrical branches

Exaggerate root system.

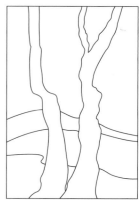
Base of tree out of lower edge of view

CONSTRUCTION

1. When you are happy with your design, transfer the design to the fusible web. Refer to Fused Segments (page 74) for instructions on how to do this. If you have a lightbox available, this will make the process much easier. Cut out the shape, leaving a small allowance around the edge.

2. Iron the fusible web to the back of the selected tree fabric. Bark can have texture, so consider choosing a fabric to replicate this.

3. Cut out the trunk on the traced line.

Iron shape drawn on fusible web to back of fabric.

Cut out trunk.

Position tree and stich in place.

4. Remove the backing paper and position the tree on the quilted background. Using a darning foot, stitch around the edges of the trees in a matching-colored thread. You can add more stitched branches if desired.

TIP • • • • • • • • • • • • • •
Superior Threads fine silk thread, size 100, which comes in heaps of colors, is perfect for this type of stitching, especially if your tree features a lot of fine branches. Use a size 8/60 needle and a fine bobbin thread.

PAINTING TRUNKS

Sometimes it is impossible to find the perfect fabric to replicate the special features of a tree. If so, trace the outline of the trunk onto white fabric and then paint the colors and textures you are trying to achieve. Use a ballpoint pen or dark sharp pencil for tracing so you can still see the outline when you paint over it. For more information on painting, refer to Creating Your Own Fabric (pages 49–56).

Paint over drawn lines.

TIP •
Iron a piece of freezer paper to the back of white fabric to provide a firm surface and stability when you are painting.

When the fabric is dry, iron to set the color. Iron a piece of fusible web to the back of the painted trunk and cut out on the drawn lines.

Remove the backing paper and position the painted tree on the quilted background. Using a darning foot, stitch around the edges of the trees in a matching-color thread.

Painted tree on background

Cut out and position trees on quilted background.

DRAWING FOLIAGE

Your tree may be a striking specimen, stripped of foliage, or even dead. If it does have a covering of leaves, it is now time to look at the various ways you can depict them. As does the trunk, the shape of the foliage contributes to the individuality and character of each species of tree.

Leaves differ enormously in size, shape, and color. The outline and the density of the canopy are the first points to consider when deciding how to portray the foliage in your design.

For some trees, it is better to think of leaf clusters rather than individual leaves. Consider the foliage as one massed shape, with clusters stacking or overlapping one another. Look at the shape of each cluster and try to reproduce this in your drawing.

Draw a lot of these shapes on fusible web and cut them out with a small seam allowance. Iron the shapes to the backs of

suitable fabrics. You can use multiple fabrics or one fabric with a variation of values and colors.

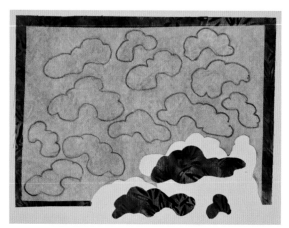

Cut out shapes and remove backing paper. Position clumps of foliage on tree branches.

Foliage on branches

Other trees feature unique foliage that can be interpreted more effectively in stitching and paint.

Painted leaves in *Fern Pool* (full quilt on page 4)

Detail of foliage portrayed as clusters in *Across the Lake* by Valerie A. Giles

Detail of foliage in *Ghost Gum on a Rocky Outcrop* (full quilt on page 38)

Detail of fabric fronds overstitched in *Howea Sunset*
by Joanne Simpson

Detail of sponged foliage in *Loddon River Tranquility*
by Gloria Loughman

Detail in diamond-shaped foliage in *Cypress at Portarlington*
(full quilt on page 22)

Abstract Trees

As you don't have to make a literal image, you can tap into your creative spirit and come up with different ways of portraying trees. You can start with the literal image and alter its design to move away from reality. The more the image is altered, the more abstract the design becomes.

Shapes can be stylized or changed, colors can be altered, and you can even ignore perspective.

Experiment and explore, moving away from the initial trunk shape. Decide what is important to retain and what you can play around with. When designing *Cypress at Portarlington* (page 22), I wanted to retain the intriguing trunk shapes, but I felt comfortable playing with the design of the foliage. The canopy was quite horizontal in appearance so the diamond tiles, positioned sideways, added a different dimension, but the trees are still recognizable to the locals.

When the background is tiled in some areas, the addition of more compatible geometric shapes can add unity to the design and provide something refreshingly different.

I have found that if you have any form of a tree in your design, it will read as a landscape. The tree, the background, or both can become more abstract in design, but the work will still have the feeling of a landscape.

Detail of small squares overlapped in *Lakeside* (full quilt on page 8)

Figures

As I find it very difficult to realistically draw faces, I resort to using silhouettes of people in my designs. A beautiful sunrise or sunset at the beach cries out for a group of figures strolling along the sand. When you are planning your quilt, think about the position of the figures and how many you want to include. Usually an odd number is more interesting than an even number, but it depends on whether you are planning the figures to represent members of your family. If you are using anonymous figures, you have a choice.

Figures created in fabric

Sunrise at Mission Beach (Australia)

Boats

Harbors have always held a special fascination for me, be it a busy modern port in a capital city or an old harbor with rustic fishing boats and colorful nets and buoys. Boats are great shapes to include as silhouettes or as interesting focal points, complete with peeling paint and rough wooden boards.

Sketch out the boats at the size that works best in your design. I sometimes find it helpful to sketch out an element and then photocopy it in different sizes. After cutting out the copies, I pin them on the background and stand back and decide which size works best.

When looking for the fabric for boats, use commercial fabrics or hand paint your own.

Boat harbor (Ireland)

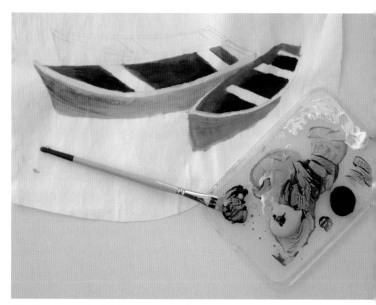

Paint boats on white fabric, cut out, and fuse.

Irish Tide by Pamela Carmody, 17″ × 22″ (43cm × 56cm)

Buildings, Bridges, and Other Man-Made Structures

HOUSES

A small building can sometimes enhance a scene, providing a focal point.

Cabin in sequoia forest (California)

The simplest design can be all that is needed. Begin with a rectangle and concentrate on the sides first before adding the roof. Playing with light against dark can allow you to add contrast and drama yet still retain the simplicity of the structure.

Power station in *Acid Rain* (full quilt on page 13)

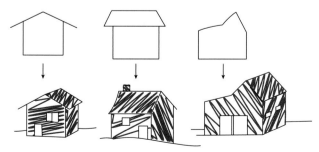

Simple shapes for buildings

WROUGHT IRON GATES

Structures such as wrought iron gates overlaid on an interesting background can create exciting visual images. By allowing the background to be featured, yet breaking it up with strong design lines, the decorative wrought iron works its magic.

Wrought iron gate

Wrought iron fence in *Parisian Promenade* (full quilt on page 30)

OTHER STRUCTURES

Wind towers, fences, lighthouses, and bridges are some of the other man-made structures that can be featured in a design. Remember to simplify the shapes and include just the essential details that are critical to the structure.

Hand-painted wind generators in *Wind Power* (full quilt on page 39)

This type of structure is cut out and fused in place on the quilted background; follow the process outlined in Trees (page 86). Use commercial fabrics, especially those that feature appropriate texture, or paint your own.

Reflections

Reflections can add something special to an image and help draw attention to the focal point. They are not the main feature, but just a pleasing illusion that adds something extra to the design. Water, wet sand, and many other smooth surfaces produce reflections. If you decide to include reflections, portray them as simply as you can, concentrating on the shape, color, and intensity.

Sunset in Tel Aviv by Lynette Linden-Simpson, 22″ × 18″ (56cm × 45cm)

Grand Mosque Sunset by Diana Knight, 26″ × 19″ (65cm × 48cm)

Stunning reflections on flooded paddocks (Murrabit, Australia)

A reflection is a mirror image of the subject being reflected. There are a number of ways to create them, including fusing fabric and stitching. A stencil technique you can use to ensure that the reflection is accurate is to trace the subject onto the shiny side of freezer paper. Cut out the image and discard it. Iron the outline stencil in position on your fabric, matching the base with the base of the subject. You can then brush paint horizontally across the stencil, knowing that the reflection will be accurate and effective.

Paint only across water area.

Simple reflection provides interest.

Rather than stitch around the outline, quilt through the reflection, keeping the stitching lines horizontal. After all, the reflection is just an illusion.

F·I·N·I·S·H·I·N·G
TECHNIQUES

Once you have quilted your design, it is time to think about the edges of the quilt. There are many options to consider. A narrow binding, a border and a binding, no border at all, multiple borders, and mounting the quilt in a solid picture frame are just some of the options. In this chapter, we will look at three of the many options you can use.

Borders can create a sense of completion and can make an image appear larger and bolder; however, unsuitable borders can really detract. Audition a range of light and dark fabrics. You will find that a dark border around a dark work will make the lighter areas stand out. Conversely, a light border around a light work will tend to highlight the darker areas. A light narrow border followed by a wider darker border can be a very effective frame for a landscape. Sometimes a border can confine a quilt too much, so consider just applying a binding or facing and having no borders at all. This will give your work a more contemporary feel, but it may not be your best option if the quilt ends up blending with the wall. Some quilts need the definition on the edge. Audition different styles of edge treatments to see which one works the best.

Regardless of how you finish your quilt, be sure to add a hanging sleeve to the back of the quilt. Use fabric that matches the backing for a professional look. Add a label with the relevant information included.

TIP • • • • • • • • • •

Fold fabric to mimic a range of border options and record the results with a digital camera. You can quickly compare images to see which border treatment enhances the quilt.

Generally, plainer fabrics such as tone-on-tones, low-contrast batiks, or hand-dyed fabrics work better for borders on landscapes. A strong patterned fabric will draw the eye out of the quilt. For the same reason, stay with the color palette of your quilt rather than introducing a new color in the border. To give some contrast, vary the value; it often works to go darker on the edge.

Small inner border with wide binding

After the Fire by Gloria Loughman, 20″ × 15″ (51cm × 38cm)

Faced edge
....
Coastal Gums by Jeannie Henry, 12″ × 16″ (31cm × 41cm)

Photo by Emilie M. Belak

Stunning border
....
Where the Bighorns Roam by Emilie M. Belak, 28″ × 28″ (71cm × 71cm)

Faced edge
....
Last Light by Gloria Loughman, 24″ × 18″ (61cm × 46cm)

Making a Faced Edge

1. Square up the quilt sandwich using a large cutting board and ruler to ensure accuracy. A large 12½″ × 12½″ (32cm × 32cm) or 15″ × 15″ (38cm × 38cm) square ruler is very useful. For this technique it is extremely important to have the quilt sandwich as square and straight as possible.

2. Measure through the vertical center length of your quilt. For the side facings, cut 2 strips 3″ (8cm) wide × the vertical center length plus 1″. With wrong sides together, press each strip in half lengthwise. (Depending on the size of your project, you may want to cut the facing strips wider than this example.)

3. Place a folded strip on the quilt front, along a side edge of the quilt, with the strip extending beyond the quilt at each end. Carefully align the raw edges and pin in position. Sew the strip to the quilt with a ¼" (6mm) seam allowance. If possible, use a walking or even-feed foot to keep even pressure on the quilt sandwich. Repeat on the other side of the quilt.

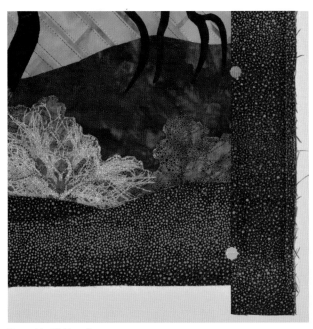

Sew with ¼" (6mm) seam.

4. Using a steam iron, press the facings flat, away from the quilt. Stitch a row of understitching ⅛" (3mm) out from the seamline.

Press facing flat, away from quilt.

5. Fold the entire facing strip on one side to the back of the quilt and press it to flatten the seam allowance. Pin; then slipstitch the folded edge to the back of the quilt. Trim each end of the facing even with the quilt. Repeat on the other side of the quilt.

Press facing to back of quilt and pin.

6. Measure through the horizontal center width of the quilt. For the top and bottom edges, cut 2 strips 3" (8cm) × the horizontal center width of the quilt plus 1" (2.5cm). With wrong sides together, press the strips in half lengthwise. Place a folded strip on the top edge of the quilt, ensuring a ½" (1.3cm) overhang at each end. Repeat Steps 3–4 to sew the facings to the top and bottom of the quilt. Fold the ends of the facing strips under, and then fold the entire facing to the back of the quilt for slipstitching down. It may be necessary to trim the bulky seam allowance in the corner a little to get a flat finish.

Allow overhang at each end.

Making a Narrow Border and Wide Binding

Quilt with narrow border and wide binding

Evening Seascape by Gloria Loughman, 25″ × 19″ (64cm × 48cm)

Picture framers often place a narrow inner border inside the large outside frame. The purpose of this inner border is to break up the movement of color flowing to the outer border. It is especially useful to break up areas of dark color in the composition that link to a dark border.

You can replicate this effect in fabric by making a ⅛″ (3mm) inside border. You can follow a simple procedure to ensure that the narrow frame is symmetrical and parallel. These instructions will create a 1″ (2.5cm) frame around your quilt.

1. Since the binding and narrow border have a combined width of 1″ (2.5cm), allow an extra 1″ (2.5cm) around the edge of the quilted top when trimming. Square up the quilt sandwich, using a large cutting board and ruler to ensure accuracy.

2. Measure the vertical center length of the quilt. For the narrow side borders, cut 2 strips 1¼″ (6mm) wide × the vertical center length plus 1″ (2.5cm). This is wider than necessary, but the extra width helps prevent stretching when the strips are applied.

3. Align a ruler along a side edge and use this as a guide for strip placement. Place the ¾″ (2cm) line of the ruler on the edge of the quilt sandwich. With right sides together, pin the narrow borders in place ¾″ (2cm) in from the edge of the quilt, with the strip ends extending beyond the quilt.

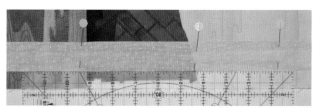

Use ruler as guide for placement.

4. Stitch these side borders with an accurate ¼" (6mm) seam and press toward the outside edge of the quilt. Trim the ends of the strips even with the quilt.

5. Measure through the horizontal center width of the quilt. For the top and bottom strips, cut 2 strips 1¼" (3cm) × the horizontal center width plus 1" (2.5 cm). Pin, attach, and trim these to the top and bottom in the same way.

Stitch narrow border and press outward.

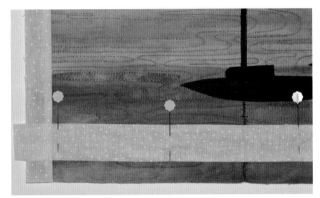

Attach top and bottom borders.

6. Cut 2 strips of outside binding fabric 4½" (11cm) wide × the vertical center length plus 1" (2.5cm). Cut 2 *additional* strips 4½" (11cm) wide × the horizontal center width plus 1" (2.5cm). Fold the strips in half lengthwise with wrong sides together and press. Pin the side binding strips in position on the quilt, with the raw edges of the strips along the ¾" (2cm) line on the ruler as a guide.

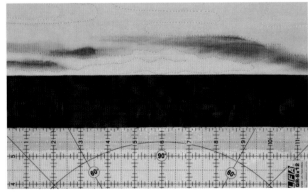

Use ¾" (2cm) line on ruler as guide for placement.

7. Turn the quilt over so that that the back of the quilt is facing up. Sew the seams from this side, either lining up the left *inside* edge of the presser foot with your initial stitching line or moving the needle position to the left as needed. The distance between the first line of stitching and the line you are stitching now should be ⅛" (3mm), the width of the narrow inside border.

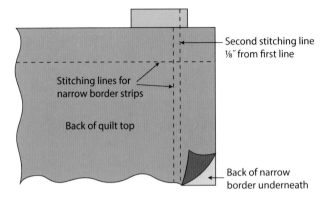

8. Press the binding toward the outside edge, fold it to the back of the quilt, and slipstitch in position. Trim the ends of the facing even with the quilt.

9. Pin the binding strips to the top and bottom of the quilt, allowing an extra ½" (1.3cm) at the ends of the top and bottom bindings to turn under when you are slipstitching the binding in place on the back of the quilt (so do not trim these ends). Repeat the stitching process in Step 8. Then press the binding toward the outside edge and fold it to the back of the quilt. Turn under the extra length and slipstitch in place.

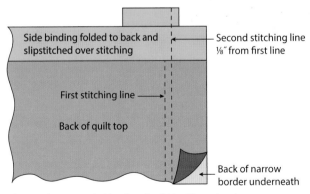

Distance between stitching lines is width of inner border.

T I P • • • • • • • • • • • • • • • • • •

Always stitch the side borders before the top and bottom so that there are no distracting vertical lines heading out the top and bottom edges of the quilt.

Making a Narrow Inner Border and Wider Outer Border Finished with a Facing

This technique combines the narrow border described in Making a Narrow Border and Wide Binding (pages 102 and 103) with a faced edge on a second wider border. The facing is applied rather than a binding, ensuring a smooth edge without the definition of a binding line. These instructions will create a narrow ⅛" (3mm) inner border with a 2⅜" (6cm) outer border.

Quilt with two borders and faced edge

Early Morning at Mission Beach by Gloria Loughman, 22½" × 31" (57cm × 79cm)

1. Trim the backing and batting, allowing a 3" (8cm) margin around the outside of the quilt top. Square up the quilt top, using a large cutting board and ruler to ensure accuracy.

2. Use 4 strips 1¼" (3cm) wide for the narrow borders. These strips need to be the length of the pieced quilt top plus 1" on each side. Follow the steps described in Making a Narrow Border and Wide Binding (pages 102 and 103) to place, stitch, and press these narrow borders on all sides of the quilt, *except* position these strips 3" (8cm) in from the outside edge of the batting and backing, using a ruler as a guide. Attach the narrow borders to the sides first and then to the top and bottom.

Pin borders in place.

Press narrow border toward outside edge.

3. Cut 2 wide border pieces 3″ × the side length of the backing and batting plus 1″ (2.5cm). Position the side border strips 3″ (8cm) from the edge of the quilt, using a ruler as a guide. Pin them in place.

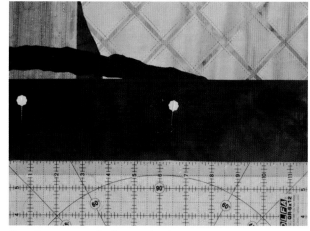

Use ruler to accurately align next border.

4. Turn the quilt over so that the back of the quilt is facing up. Sew the borders, following the instructions outlined in Step 7 (page 103) for stitching the binding. Press the borders toward the outside edge of the quilt.

5. Cut the top and bottom border strips and add them in the same way as Step 4.

6. Trim all the border pieces even with the quilt backing. Check the accuracy of the quilt. You have the opportunity to square it up again at this stage, but be sure you are keeping the quilt centered in its frame. At this time you may trim the outside border to a narrower width if desired.

7. Add a facing to the outside edges, following the steps in Making a Faced Edge (pages 100 and 101).

Press border toward outside edge.

The Baobab Trees of Madagascar

Finished size: 20″ × 30″ (51cm × 76cm)

FABRIC REQUIREMENTS

BASE FABRIC: ⅔ yard (65cm) to be placed under tiles

TILE FABRIC: ½ yard (46cm) of multicolored fabric *or* 4–5 fat quarters of fabrics that blend

FOREGROUND:
⅛ yard (15cm) of green fabric
⅓ yard (30cm) of brown fabric

BACKGROUND TREES:
⅛ yard (15cm) of green fabric
⅛ yard (15cm) of orange-green fabric

BAOBAB TREES:
½ yard (46cm) of dark violet fabric

FACING: ⅝ yard (58cm)

BACKING: 24″ × 34″ (61cm × 86cm)

OTHER SUPPLIES

FREEZER PAPER: 1½ yards (1.5m)

PAPER-BACKED FUSIBLE WEB:
1½ yards (1.5m) of 24″-wide (61cm-wide) Lite Steam-A-Seam 2 (or similar)

BATTING: 24″ × 34″ (61cm × 86cm)

THREAD:
• to blend with tiles
• to match trees

INVISIBLE THREAD:
nylon or polyester

This small wallhanging features a background of rectangular tiles, described in detail in Constructing the Background (pages 57–74).

Getting Started

1. Use a copy machine to enlarge the project pattern (page 110) 300%.

2. Trace Segment 1 (including Fused Segments 2, 2A, and 3) onto the dull side of the freezer paper. Trace Segments 4 and 5 individually. Include the numbers on each segment. Cut out each freezer-paper segment.

3. Iron the freezer-paper pattern for Segment 1 onto the right side of the selected sky background fabric. Cut it out with a generous 1″ (2.5cm) seam allowance around the outside of the freezer paper.

4. Select fabrics for the rectangular tiles. The selection can include a number of different fabrics or one fabric with interesting changes in color. Follow the manufacturer's instructions to iron paper-backed fusible web, such as Lite Steam-A-Seam 2, to the back of the chosen fabrics.

TIP •
Lite Steam-A-Seam 2 has an adhesive on both sides of the fusible web, allowing the mosaic pieces to adhere to the background before ironing. Other fusible webs, such as Wonder Under, have paper backing on only one side and no adhesive.

5. Leaving one side of the backing paper of the fusible web still attached, rotary cut the fabric backed with fusible web into rectangles ¾″ × 2″ (2cm × 5cm). Refer to Cutting Rectangular Tiles (page 59) as needed.

6. Position the 45° line of a rotary cutting ruler along the right edge of the sky base fabric and draw some guide lines.

7. Following the instructions in Rectangular Tiles in the Sky (pages 64–66), position the tiles on the sky background fabric. When you are happy with the placement, remove the backing paper and iron to adhere the tiles permanently.

Place tiles in position.

Stitching the Tiles

1. Sandwich the sky fabric, batting, and backing, lining up the top edge and left side edge. Pin the layers together using safety pins or straight pins.

2. Using a walking foot if available, stitch down both sides of the tiles. Begin at the top left-hand corner. Stitch approximately ⅛″ (3mm) in from the edges of the tiles and continue down to the bottom of each row. Refer to Stitching Down the Tiles (pages 69–71) as needed.

Background Foliage

1. Refer to Fused Segments (page 74) to trace Fused Segments 2, 2A, and 3 onto fusible web. (Trace on the paper liner that stays with the web.) To avoid creating a mirror image, trace from the back of the pattern using a lightbox or window. Cut the segments out with a small allowance around each shape, and press the fusible web to the back of the selected foliage fabrics. Cut out the shapes on the lines, allowing extra fabric on the side and bottom edges as a seam allowance to tuck under the next segments.

Allow seam allowance on lower edge.

2. Remove the backing paper and position the foliage on the quilt top, referring to the pattern as a guide for placement. Place Fused Segments 2 and 2A in position first as the back row, and then add Fused Segment 3 as the front row. Press the foliage permanently to the background. Stitch along the top edges of the foliage with a matching thread.

Back row of foliage in position

Front row added

Lower Section of the Landscape

1. Press freezer-paper Segments 4 and 5 onto the right side of the fabrics selected for the lower sections of the landscape. Cut them out with a ½" (1.3cm) seam allowance around each segment.

2. Keeping the freezer paper on the fabric, trim the top-edge seam allowance of each section to ¼" (6mm) and press the seam allowance to the back.

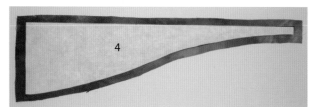

Cut out with seam allowance.

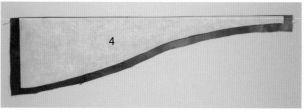

Press top-edge seam allowance to back.

3. Remove the freezer paper and position Segment 4 on the quilt sandwich, using the pattern as a guide for placement. Pin the segment in place.

4. Stitch Segment 4 in position using the blind hem stitch on your sewing machine. Use a clear invisible thread on the top and a matching-colored thread in the bobbin. Refer to Invisible Appliqué (page 73).

5. Add quilting lines to Segment 4, referring to Quilting the Landscape Details (page 74).

Foreground Highlights

1. Refer to Fused Segments (page 74) to trace the individual baobab trees onto fusible web. (Trace on the paper liner that stays with the web.) To avoid creating a mirror image, trace from the back of the pattern using a lightbox or window. Cut out the shapes drawn on the fusible web, leaving a small allowance around the edge of each shape.

2. Iron the fusible web to the back of the selected tree fabrics. Cut out on the traced lines.

3. Remove the backing paper and position only the 4 smaller trees on the quilt sandwich. Do not position the large foreground tree at this stage. Press the trees in place. Stitch around the edges of the trees in a matching-colored thread. Add more stitched branches if desired.

4. Prepare Segment 5 (foreground) following the instructions for Segment 4. Place the segment in position on the quilt top and stitch in place using the invisible blind hem stitch.

5. Remove the backing paper from the large baobab tree and position it in place. Press the tree permanently in place and stitch around the edges using a matching-colored thread.

6. Stitch grass around the base of the trees.

Faced Edge

1. Square up the quilt using a large cutting board and ruler to ensure accuracy. A 12½″ square ruler is very useful for this purpose.

2. Cut and apply 5″ (13cm) strips for the facing, following the instructions in Making a Faced Edge (pages 100 and 101).

3. Add a sleeve and label.

Segment 4 pinned in place.

Baobab trees cut out and ready to be positioned

The Baobab Trees of Madagascar

Enlarge 300%.

1

Fused 2

Fused 3

Fused 2A

4

5

The Cypress Trees of Florida

Finished size: 17″ × 27″ (43cm × 69cm)

This small wallhanging features a background of squares, described in Constructing the Background (pages 57–74).

FABRIC REQUIREMENTS

BASE FABRIC:
19″ × 21″ (48cm × 53cm)
to be placed under tiles

TILES: ½ yard (46cm) of
multicolored fabric *or* 4–5 fat
quarters of fabrics that blend

WATER IN FOREGROUND:
⅓ yard (31cm)

TREE LINE IN BACKGROUND:
⅛ yard (11cm)

CYPRESS TREES: ½ yard (46cm)

NARROW BORDER:
⅙ yard (15cm)

BINDING: ⅓ yard (31cm)

BACKING:
21″ × 31″ (53cm × 79cm)

OTHER SUPPLIES

FREEZER PAPER: 1 yard (1m)

PAPER-BACKED FUSIBLE WEB:
1 yard (1m) of 24″-wide (61cm-wide)
Lite Steam-A-Seam 2 (or similar)

BATTING: 21″ × 31″
(53cm × 79cm)

THREADS:
  • to blend with tiles
    • to match cypress trees
    • to match water

INVISIBLE THREAD:
nylon or polyester

Getting Started

1. Use a copy machine to enlarge the project pattern (page 115) 300%.

2. Trace the background Segment 1 (trace Segment 1 so it includes Fused Segment 2) and Segment 3 onto the dull side of the freezer paper. Include the number on each segment. Cut out each freezer-paper segment.

3. Iron the freezer-paper pattern for Segment 1 onto the right side of the selected sky base fabric. Cut it out with a generous 1″ (2.5cm) seam allowance around the outside of the freezer paper.

Base fabric

4. Select fabrics for the square tiles. The selection can include a number of different fabrics, as shown, or one fabric with interesting changes in color. Follow the manufacturer's instructions to iron paper-backed fusible web to the back of the chosen fabrics.

Selection of fabric for tiles

5. Leaving the backing paper of the fusible web in place, rotary cut the fabric backed with fusible web into 1½″ × 1½″ (3.8cm × 3.8cm) squares. Refer to Cutting Square Tiles (page 60) as needed.

6. Position the 45° line of a rotary cutting ruler along the right edge of the sky base fabric and draw some lines. Refer to Square Tiles in the Sky (page 66).

Draw guidelines on sky base fabric.

7. Following the instructions in Square Tiles in the Sky (pages 66 and 67), position the square tiles on the sky base fabric. When you are happy with the placement, remove the backing paper and iron to adhere the tiles permanently.

Place tiles in position.

Stitching the Tiles

1. Trim the batting and backing fabric to 18½″ × 28½″ (47cm × 72cm). Sandwich the sky fabric, batting, and backing, with the sky centered 1″ (2.5cm) in from the top and side edges. Pin the layers together using safety pins or straight pins.

2. Using a walking foot if available, stitch down both sides of the tiles. Begin at the top left-hand corner, stitching approximately ⅛″ (3mm) in from the edges of the tiles. Continue down to the bottom of each row, run along the bottom edge, and then stitch back up the other side of the row. Refer to Stitching Down the Tiles (pages 69–72) as needed.

Background Trees

1. Refer to Fused Segments (page 74) to trace the distant tree line (Fused Segment 2) onto fusible web. (Trace on the paper liner that stays with the web.) To avoid creating a mirror image, trace from the back of the pattern using a lightbox or window. Cut out the shape with a small margin and then press the fusible web to the back of the selected tree fabric. Cut out the shape on the line, allowing extra fabric on the side and bottom edges as a seam allowance to tuck under the water segment.

Cut out distant tree line.

2. Remove the backing paper and press the shape in position on the quilted sky. Stitch along the top edge of the tree line with a matching-colored thread.

Lower Section of Landscape

1. Press the Segment 3 freezer-paper pattern onto the right side of the water fabric. Cut out the water segment with a ½″ (1.3cm) seam allowance around the edge of the freezer paper.

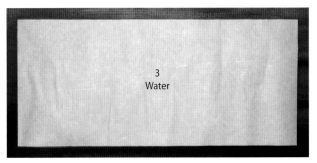
Cut out water segment with ½″ seam allowance.

2. Keeping the freezer paper in place, trim the seam allowance along the segment's top edge to ¼″ (6mm) and press this seam allowance to the back.

3. Remove the freezer paper and position Segment 3 onto the quilt sandwich, using the pattern as a guide for placement. Pin the water in place.

Water pinned in position and ready to be stitched

4. Stitch along the top edge using the blind hem stitch (page 73) on your sewing machine. Use a clear invisible thread on the top and a matching-colored thread in the bobbin.

5. Add quilting lines to the water segment. Refer to Quilting the Landscape Details (page 74).

Suggested quilting lines for water

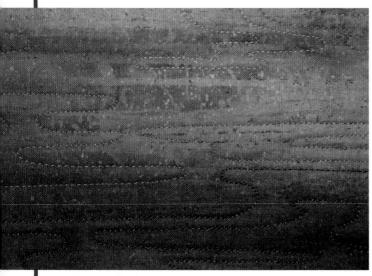

Close-up of quilting

Foreground Highlights

1. Refer to Fused Segments (page 74) to trace the individual cypress trees onto fusible web. (Trace on the paper that stays with the web.) To avoid creating a mirror image, trace from the back of the pattern using a lightbox or window. Cut out the images, leaving a small allowance around the edge of each shape. *Note: Feel free to change or simplify the trees if you are concerned about stitching the fine details.*

2. Iron the fusible web to the back of the selected tree fabric. Cut out the trees on the traced lines.

Cypress trees cut out and ready to be positioned

3. Refer to the project photo (page 111) to position the trees on the quilt sandwich. Remove the backing paper and press the trees in place. Stitch around the edges of the trees in a matching-colored thread. I would suggest that you use a very fine thread and fine needle so you can stitch the fragile tree edges without breaking them.

Finishing Your Quilt

1. Square up the quilt using a large cutting board and ruler to ensure accuracy, allowing an extra 1" (2.5 cm) around the edge of the quilt top when trimming.

2. Cut 3 strips 1¼" (3cm) wide for narrow borders and 3 strips 4½" (11 cm) wide for the binding. Cut 1 of each strip in half for the top and bottom borders and bindings.

3. Add the border and binding as outlined in Making a Narrow Border and Wide Binding (pages 102 and 103).

4. Add a sleeve and label.

The Cypress Trees of Florida
Enlarge 300%.

1

Fused 2

3

The Pines of Norfolk Island

Finished size: 28½″ × 21″ (73cm × 53cm)

This small wallhanging features a sky of diamond mosaics, as described in Constructing the Background (pages 57–74). The fabrics for the sky were hand painted and then cut into tiles. You can paint or dye your own fabric, following the instructions in Creating Your Own Fabric (pages 49–56), or use commercial fabrics for this quilt.

Getting Started

1. Use a copy machine to enlarge the project pattern (page 121) 250%.

2. Trace the background Segments 1 (trace Segment 1 to include Fused Segment 2), 3, 4, and 5 onto the dull side of the freezer paper. The pattern has bold lines defining these segments. Include the number on each segment. Cut out each freezer-paper segment.

3. Iron the freezer-paper pattern for the sky segment (Segment 1) onto the right side of the selected sky background fabric. Cut this out with a generous 1″ (2.5cm) seam allowance around the outside of the freezer paper.

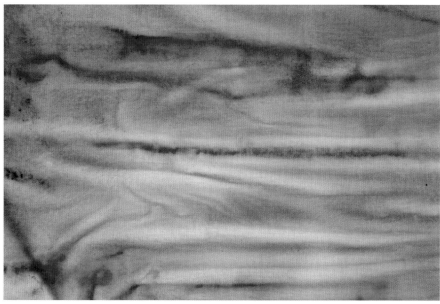

Sky base fabric

4. Select fabrics for the diamond tiles. The selection can include a number of different fabrics or one fabric with interesting changes in color.

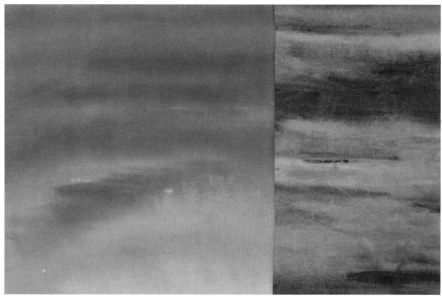

Selection of hand-painted fabrics for diamond tiles

FABRIC REQUIREMENTS

BASE FABRIC: ½ yard (46cm) to be placed under tiles

TILES: ½ yard (46cm) of multicolored fabric *or* 3–4 fat quarters of sky fabric that blends

SEA: ⅙ yard (15cm)

MIDDLE AREA OF LAND: ⅙ yard (15cm)

LAND IN FOREGROUND: ⅙ yard (15cm)

SMALL TREES IN MIDGROUND: ⅙ yard (15cm)

LARGE TREE: ¼ yard (25cm) of dark green

ROCKY ISLAND: small pieces

SMALL BUILDINGS: small pieces

ROOFS: small pieces

BACKING: 33″ × 25″ (83cm × 64cm)

NARROW BORDER: ¼ yard (23cm)

WIDER OUTSIDE BORDER: ½ yard (46cm)

FACING: ½ yard (46cm)

OTHER SUPPLIES

FREEZER PAPER: 1 yard (1m)

FUSIBLE WEB: 1 yard (1m) of 24″-wide (61cm-wide) Lite Steam-A-Seam 2 (or similar)

BATTING: 33″ × 25″ (83cm × 64cm)

THREADS:
- to blend with tiles
- to match background trees, buildings, and large foreground tree
- to quilt water and land

INVISIBLE THREAD: nylon or polyester

DARK FABRIC MARKING PEN

5. Referring to Cutting Diamond Tiles (pages 60–62), draw diamond tiles on the smooth side of the fusible web. Use the measurement of 1½" (3.8cm) for the strips. Follow the manufacturer's instructions to iron the fusible web to the back of the chosen fabrics. If a fabric has lines, make sure they are positioned along the horizontal width of the diamond.

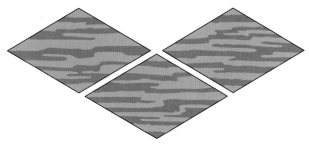

Lines placed along horizontal width

6. Using the drawn lines on the fusible web as a guide, cut the fabric backed with fusible web into diamonds. You can use a rotary cutter or scissors.

7. Refer to Cutting Diamond Tiles (page 60) to draw guidelines on the sky base fabric. Position the 60° line of a rotary cutting ruler along the right edge of the fabric and draw some guidelines with a fabric pencil or chalk.

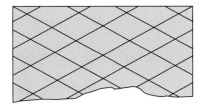

Draw guidelines on sky base fabric.

8. Following the instructions in Diamonds in the Sky (page 68), position the diamond tiles on the sky base fabric. When you are happy with the placement, remove the backing paper and iron to adhere the tiles permanently.

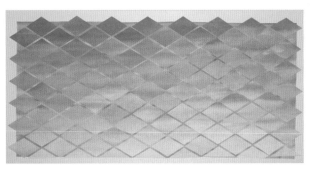

Place tiles in position.

Stitching the Tiles

1. Trim the batting and backing fabric to 30" × 22½" (76cm × 57cm). This is larger than the pattern to allow for borders later in the process. Sandwich the sky fabric, batting, and backing, with the sky positioned 3" (8cm) in from the top and left side edges. Pin the layers together using safety pins or straight pins.

2. Choose a thread that blends well with the tile fabrics. Using a walking foot if available, stitch down both sides of the tiles. Begin at the top left-hand corner, stitching approximately ⅛" (3mm) in from the edges of the tiles. Continue down to the bottom of each row, run along the bottom edge, and then stitch back up the other side of the row. Refer to Stitching Down the Tiles (pages 69–72) as needed.

Island

1. Refer to Fused Segments (page 74) to trace the rocky island (Fused Segment 2) onto fusible web. (Trace on the paper that stays with the web.) To avoid creating a mirror image, trace from the back of the pattern using a lightbox or window. Cut out the island with a small margin and then press the fusible web to the back of the island fabric. Cut out the shape on the line but allow a small seam allowance on the bottom edge to tuck under the sea segment.

2. Remove the backing paper and position the island on the quilted sky, referring to the pattern for accurate placement. Stitch along the top edge of the island with a matching thread.

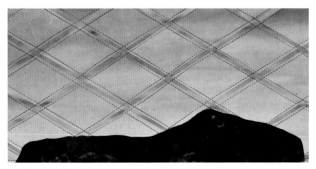

Position island on sky.

Water and Land Segments

1. Press freezer-paper Segment 3 to the right side of the water fabric. Cut out the water segment with a ½" (1.3cm) seam allowance around the edge of the freezer paper. Press freezer-paper Segments 4 and 5 to the right sides of the selected fabrics and cut out with ½" seam allowances. Fabric for Segment 5 can have more texture and can be more saturated with color, as it is in the foreground.

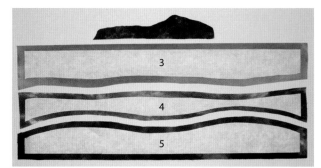

Foreground and segments cut out with seam allowances

2. Keeping the freezer paper in position, trim the top-edge seam allowance of each section to ¼" (6mm) and press this seam allowance to the back.

3. Remove the freezer paper and position Segment 3 on the quilt sandwich, using the pattern as a guide for placement. Pin the water in place.

Water pinned in position and ready to be stitched

4. Stitch along the top edge using the blind hem stitch (page 73) on your sewing machine. Use a clear invisible thread on the top and a matching-colored thread in the bobbin.

5. Repeat this process for Segment 4.

Small Trees, Buildings, and Hedges

1. As in Fused Segments (page 74), trace the individual pine trees from the pattern onto fusible web. (Trace on the paper that stays with the web.) Cut out the images, leaving a small allowance around the edge of each shape. Feel free to change or simplify the trees if you are concerned about stitching the fine details. Repeat this process with the hedges and buildings, tracing the roof and wall sections separately. Add a small seam allowance to the top edges of the walls to go under the roof and allow a small allowance on the bottom edges as needed.

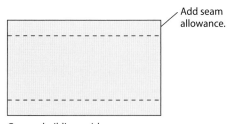

Add seam allowance.

Cut out buildings with seam allowance on top edge.

2. Iron the fusible web to the back of the selected tree, building, and hedge fabrics. Cut out the shapes on the traced lines.

3. Save the largest tree to be positioned later. Remove the fusible-web backing paper and, referring to the pattern, position the 5 small trees and the base of the buildings on the quilt sandwich. Iron to adhere the shapes permanently and then stitch around the edges using a matching thread.

Small trees with part of buildings in place

4. In a similar manner, add the roofs to the buildings and
the hedges.

Add roofs and hedges.

Foreground Highlights

Remove the freezer paper on Segment 5 and position this
on the quilt sandwich, using the pattern as a guide for
placement. Pin this section of land in place and stitch using
the blind hem stitch.

Segment 5 in position

Large Tree and Building Details

1. Remove the fusible-web backing paper and position
the largest tree on the quilt sandwich. Use a darning foot
to free-motion stitch around the edges of the trees in a
matching-colored thread. You can add extra stitching to
show the texture of the pine needles or leave as a simplified
fabric outline.

2. Use a dark fabric marking pen to add the remaining
building details (windows and so on).

Tree stitched in place and windows added

Finishing Your Quilt

1. Square up the quilt using a large cutting board and ruler
to ensure accuracy. Allow an extra 3″ (8cm) around the
outside of the quilt top.

2. Follow the steps outlined in Making a Narrow Inner
Border and Wider Outer Border Finished with a Facing
(pages 104 and 105) to add the borders and facing to
the quilt.

Cut 4 strips 1¼″ (3cm) wide for the narrow borders, 4 strips
3″ (8cm) wide for the larger outside border, and 4 strips
3″ (8cm) wide for the facing.

3. Add a sleeve and label.

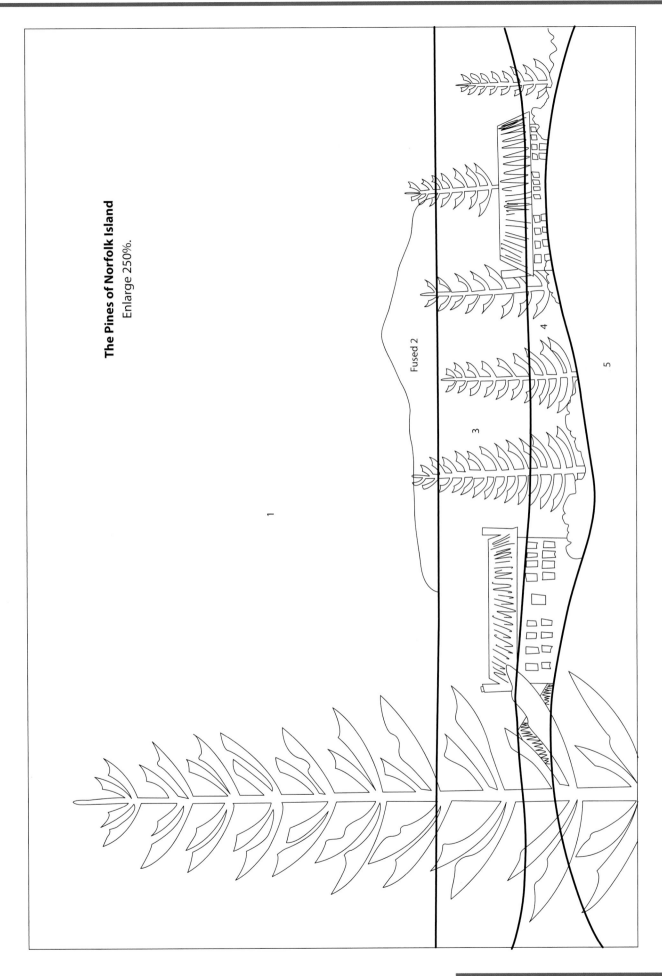

The Pines of Norfolk Island
Enlarge 250%.

Fused 2

1

3

4

5

Aspen Forest

Finished size: 21″ × 40″ (53cm × 102cm)

FABRIC REQUIREMENTS

BACKGROUND: 1¼ yards (1.2m) to be placed under tiles

TILES: 6–8 fat eighths (choose a variety of textures and values, including at least 1 highlight fabric)

TREE TRUNKS: 1½ yards (1.5m)

SMALLER BRANCHES IN FRONT: ½ yard (46cm) (more intense in color than trunks)

LEAVES: small pieces with a variety of colors

FACING: ⅔ yard (61cm)

BACKING: 25″ × 44″ (64cm × 112cm)

OTHER SUPPLIES

FUSIBLE WEB: 4 yards (2m) of 24″-wide (61cm-wide) Lite Steam-A-Seam 2 (or similar) for background, tree trunks, branches, and leaves

BATTING: 25″ × 44″ (64cm × 112cm)

THREADS:
- to blend with tiles
- to match tree trunks
- to match leaves (variegated thread to blend with leaf colors recommended)

This rectangular wallhanging features a background of rectangular tiles, described in detail in Constructing the Background (starting on page 57). More information about creating the trees can be found in Trees (page 86).

Getting Started

1. Use a copy machine to enlarge the project pattern (page 126) 400% and to enlarge the following leaf pattern 200%.

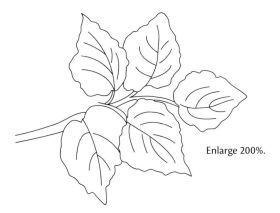

Enlarge 200%.

2. Cut a 24″ × 43″ (61cm × 110cm) rectangle from the background fabric.

3. Select fabrics for the rectangular tiles. Make sure you include different values as well as some brighter colors for highlights. Follow the manufacturer's instructions to iron paper-backed fusible web to the back of the chosen fabrics.

TIP •

Lite Steam-A-Seam 2 has an adhesive on both sides of the fusible web, allowing the mosaic pieces to adhere to the background before ironing. Other fusible webs, such as Wonder Under, have paper backing on only one side and no adhesive.

4. Leaving the backing paper of the fusible web still attached, rotary cut the fabric backed with fusible web into rectangles ¾″ × 2″ (2cm × 5cm). Refer to Cutting Rectangular Tiles (page 59) as needed.

5. Use a ruler and chalk or marking pencil to draw a line parallel to a long edge of the background fabric. Draw additional parallel lines about 3″ apart across the background piece. Refer to Placing the Tiles (page 64).

6. Position the tiles on the sky background fabric. When you are happy with the placement, remove the backing paper and press to adhere the tiles permanently in place.

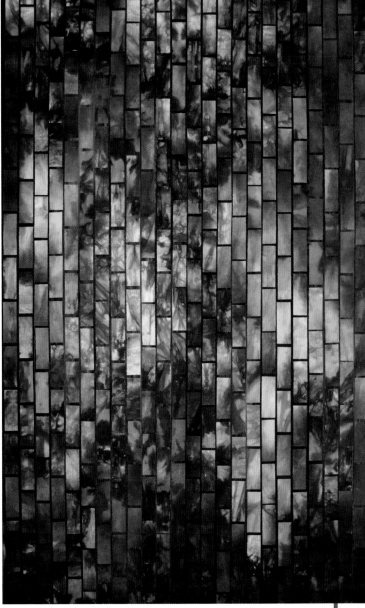

Add tiles until background is covered.

Stitching the Tiles

1. Cut the backing fabric and batting to 24″ × 43″ (61cm × 110cm). Sandwich the tiled background fabric, batting, and backing, lining up the top edge and left side edge. Pin the layers together using safety pins or straight pins.

2. Using a walking foot if available, stitch down both sides of the tiles. Begin at the top left-hand corner. Stitch approximately ⅛″ (3mm) in from the edges of the tiles and continue down to the bottom of each row. Refer to Stitching Down the Tiles (pages 69–71) as needed.

Trunks and Branches

1. Refer to Fused Segments (page 74) to trace the tree trunks and smaller branches individually onto fusible web. (Trace on the paper that stays with the web.) To avoid creating a mirror image, trace from the back of the pattern using a lightbox or window. If you plan to paint the tree trunks on white cotton fabric, refer to Painting Trunks (pages 89 and 90). The foreground branches are cut out separately.

2. Cut out the shapes drawn on the fusible web, leaving a small allowance around the edges.

3. Iron these fusible web shapes to the back of the selected trunk and branch fabrics.

4. Cut out the trunks and branches on the traced lines.

5. Remove the backing paper and position the trunks on the forest background. Press into place permanently.

6. Stitch around the edge of each trunk in a matching thread. At this stage you have the opportunity to add further stitching to create more texture and perspective.

7. Remove the backing paper and position the branches in the foreground. Iron in position. Stitch around the edges using a matching-colored thread.

Stitch around edges in matching thread.

Add foreground branches.

Place tree trunks in position.

Leaves

1. As above, trace the leaf shapes onto the smooth side of fusible web. Cut out groups of leaves, leaving a small margin around the outside. Iron the fusible web to the back of the selected leaf fabrics. Cut out individual leaves.

Cut out leaves backed with fusible web.

2. Remove the backing paper from the leaves and arrange them on the branches.

Arrange clusters of leaves on branches.

3. Iron to adhere and then stitch around the edge of each leaf. Stitch in veins to add extra texture. A variegated thread is a good choice for stitching multicolored leaves.

Stitch veins and around edges of leaves.

Finishing Your Quilt

1. Square up the quilt using a large cutting board and ruler to ensure an accurate rectangle.

2. Cut strips 5" (13cm) wide for the facing. Apply the facing as outlined in Making a Faced Edge (pages 100 and 101).

3. Add a sleeve and label.

Aspen Forest
Enlarge 400%.

About the Author

Gloria Loughman lives by the sea on the beautiful Bellarine Peninsula in Victoria, Australia. Married with three daughters, she is a trained secondary teacher, having worked mainly in literacy and special education faculties. Her initiation into the world of patchwork occurred approximately 24 years ago, when she was recovering from surgery and chemotherapy for breast cancer.

Over the years she has dabbled in many areas, including strip piecing, bargello, colorwash, fabric dyeing and painting, and machine embroidery. After completing studies in design and color as part of a Diploma of Art in 1996, she began to make her large vivid landscape quilts depicting the Australian bush. These quilts have won many major awards in Australia, Europe, Japan, and the United States. Her quilt *Kimberley Mystique* was the winner of Australia's most prestigious national quilting award in 2003.

Gloria loves sharing her knowledge and skills with others. Known to take people outside their comfort zone, Gloria is adept at pushing boundaries while still managing to instill confidence. Many students come back for a second or third class. Gloria's commitment to teaching was acknowledged by her receiving the 2009 Rajah Award for her outstanding contribution to quilt-making in Australia.

In addition to being in demand as a teacher, Gloria has curated twelve exhibitions of Australian quilts in the United States and has had the privilege of judging at many major shows. Her work has been featured in many books and magazines.

What began as a therapy has developed into a passion and has given Gloria the opportunity to travel the world, exhibiting her quilts, teaching classes, and meeting a lot of wonderful people.

Gloria's website: www.glorialoughman.com

Also by Gloria Loughman:

Great Titles *from* C&T PUBLISHING

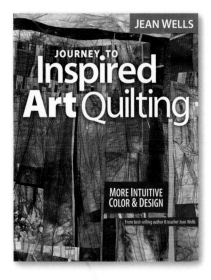

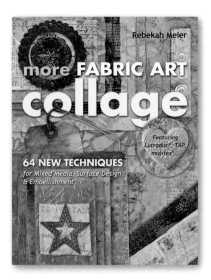

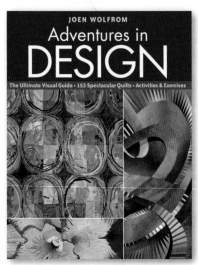

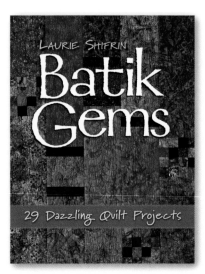

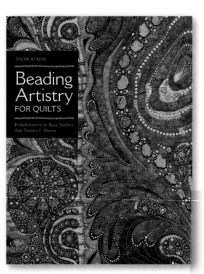

Available at your local retailer or **www.ctpub.com** *or* **800-284-1114**

For a list of other fine books from C&T Publishing, visit our website to view our catalog online.

C&T PUBLISHING, INC.
P.O. Box 1456
Lafayette, CA 94549
800-284-1114

Email: ctinfo@ctpub.com
Website: www.ctpub.com

C&T Publishing's professional photography services are now available to the public. Visit us at www.ctmediaservices.com.

Tips and Techniques can be found at www.ctpub.com > Consumer Resources > Quiltmaking Basics: Tips & Techniques for Quiltmaking & More

For quilting supplies:

COTTON PATCH
1025 Brown Ave.
Lafayette, CA 94549
Store: 925-284-1177
Mail order: 925-283-7883

Email: CottonPa@aol.com
Website: www.quiltusa.com

Note: Fabrics shown may not be currently available, as fabric manufacturers keep most fabrics in print for only a short time.